T0310642

Mastering Swift

Mastering Computer Science
Series Editor: Sufyan bin Uzayr

Mastering Swift: A Beginner's Guide
Mathew Rooney and Madina Karybzhanova

Mastering C++: A Beginner's Guide
Divya Sachdeva and Natalya Ustukpayeva

Mastering Git: A Beginner's Guide
Sumanna Kaul, Shahryar Raz, and Divya Sachdeva

Mastering Java: A Beginner's Guide
Divya Sachdeva and Natalya Ustukpayeva

Mastering Ruby on Rails: A Beginner's Guide
Mathew Rooney and Madina Karybzhanova

Mastering Sketch: A Beginner's Guide
Mathew Rooney and Md Javed Khan

For more information about this series, please visit: https://www.routledge.com/Mastering-Computer-Science/book-series/MCS

The "Mastering Computer Science" series of books are authored by the Zeba Academy team members, led by Sufyan bin Uzayr.

Zeba Academy is an EdTech venture that develops courses and content for learners primarily in STEM fields, and offers education consulting to Universities and Institutions worldwide. For more info, please visit https://zeba.academy

Mastering Swift

A Beginner's Guide

Edited by Sufyan bin Uzayr

CRC Press
Taylor & Francis Group
Boca Raton London New York

CRC Press is an imprint of the
Taylor & Francis Group, an **informa** business

First edition published 2022
by CRC Press
6000 Broken Sound Parkway NW, Suite 300, Boca Raton, FL 33487-2742

and by CRC Press
2 Park Square, Milton Park, Abingdon, Oxon, OX14 4RN

CRC Press is an imprint of Taylor & Francis Group, LLC

© 2022 Sufyan bin Uzayr

ISBN: 9781032183404 (hbk)
ISBN: 9781032182612 (pbk)
ISBN: 9781003254089 (ebk)

DOI: 10.1201/9781003254089

Typeset in Minion
by KnowledgeWorks Global Ltd.

Contents

About the Editor

Sufyan bin Uzayr is a writer, coder and entrepreneur with more than a decade of experience in the industry. He has authored several books in the past, pertaining to a diverse range of topics, ranging from History to Computers/IT.

Sufyan is the Director of Parakozm, a multinational IT company specializing in EdTech solutions. He also runs Zeba Academy, an online learning and teaching vertical with a focus on STEM fields.

Sufyan specializes in a wide variety of technologies, such as JavaScript, Dart, WordPress, Drupal, Linux and Python. He holds multiple degrees, including ones in Management, IT, Literature and Political Science.

Sufyan is a digital nomad, dividing his time between four countries. He has lived and taught in universities and educational institutions around the globe. Sufyan takes a keen interest in technology, politics, literature, history and sports, and in his spare time, he enjoys teaching coding and English to young students.

Learn more at sufyanism.com.

CHAPTER 1

Introduction to Swift Programming Language

IN THIS CHAPTER

➤ Getting to know the history of the Swift programming language

➤ Learning about Swift major benefits and technical requirements

➤ Understanding Swift Installation procedure

Swift is a great way to write software, whether it is for phones, desktops, servers, or anything else that runs code. It is a safe, fast, and immersive programming language that combines the best tools and methods in modern language

DOI: 10.1201/9781003254089-1

thinking with high standards from the wider Apple engineering culture and the diverse contributions from its open-source community. The compiler is enhanced for performance, and the language is enhanced for development, without having to compromise on either.

In case you are a beginner, there is no need to worry because Swift is extremely friendly to new programmers. Since it is an industrial-quality programming language it is expressive and enjoyable as a scripting language. Trying Swift code in a playground will let you experiment with code and see the results immediately, without the overhead of building and operating an app.

At its core, Swift is a general-purpose, multi-paradigm programming language developed by Apple Inc. and the open-source community. First released in 2014, Swift was developed as a replacement for Apple's earlier programming language Objective-C, as Objective-C had been largely unmodified since the early 1980s and lacked modern language features. Swift works with Apple's Cocoa and Cocoa Touch frameworks, and a key aspect of Swift's design was the capacity to interoperate with the huge body of existing Objective-C code developed for Apple products over the previous decades. On Apple platforms, it uses the Objective-C runtime library which allows C, Objective-C, C++, and Swift code to run within one program.

Initially, Apple intended Swift to support many core concepts associated with Objective-C, notably dynamic dispatch, widespread late binding, extensible programming, and similar features, but in a consistent way, therefore, making it easier to catch software bugs. Swift was advanced with some other features addressing common programming errors like null pointer dereferencing and provides syntactic sugar to help prevent the pyramid of doom. Swift can define large classes of common programming errors simply by adopting the following modern programming patterns:

- Memory is managed automatically.

- Error handling allows controlled recovery from unexpected failures.

- Variables are always initialized before use.

- Array indices are checked for out-of-bounds errors.

- Integers values are checked for overflow.

- Optional values ensure that nil values are managed explicitly.

In addition, Swift also supports the concept of protocol extensibility, an extensibility system that can be applied to types, structures, and classes, which Apple promotes as a real change in programming paradigms they name "protocol-oriented programming." At the same time, Swift code is compiled and improved to get the most out of its modern hardware. The syntax core and standard library have been built based on the guiding principle that the easiest way to write your code should also perform the best. Its combination of safety and speed make Swift an obvious choice for everything starting from "Hello, world!" to an entire operating system.

Moreover, Swift has powerful type inference and pattern matching with a flexible, lightweight syntax, allowing complex ideas to be realized in a clear and concise manner. As a result, code is not just easier to write, but easier to insert and maintain as well. We should also remember that Swift has been years in the making, and it still continues to evolve with new features and competencies. And while we tend to hear about programming languages like Python and JavaScript all the time, Swift is a language that is slightly less popular and a bit more niche. However, this does not mean that it is less important—it is the main programming language for a large variety of Apple devices.

In this chapter, we will introduce you to Swift, its past and its future, and give you reasons why you should start thinking about learning the language and building Swift projects. Overall, this book will hopefully prepare you for more extensive iOS app development and build a foundation for advanced iOS development designs. Upon completing this Mastering piece, you will be able to:

1. develop the ability to read and write Swift code;

2. distinguish how both programming languages can be used together in applications;

3. demonstrate how to write applications entirely in Swift with the help from several iOS programming samples;

4. associate the relationship of Swift and Objective-C and their use in iOS and Mac programming; and

5. determine how Swift can be used for development on new platforms.

WHAT IS SWIFT

Swift is a powerful general-purpose programming language serving mainly the Apple ecosystem. Whether you need to develop for iOS or any of the surrounding operating systems like macOS, tvOS, and others, Swift will be one of the main tools in your toolset.

As previously mentioned, Swift's focus is safety and clarity. By design, Swift eliminates certain classes of unsafe code that are still allowed in languages like JavaScript. Thus, it enables developers to catch some bugs at compile time before delivering them to the user community.

On the other side, Swift's clear and expressive syntax enables developers to create more compact programs than in languages like Java or C++. And even if it is being applied mainly for Apple products, Swift has recently got some market share in areas like machine learning and web. For instance, a popular end-to-end open-source platform for machine learning called TensorFlow added Swift support because of the increased speed and type safety over Python.

A Brief History of Swift

The development of Swift started back in 2010. At that time, Chris Lattner (the creator of LLVM compiler front end for the C, C++, Objective-C, and Objective-C++ programming languages) had just announced adding C++ support for Clang, a compiler for the C-like language family. Being focused on C for a long time, he decided to check whether there was a better way of doing development. And just like that, together with Bertrand Serlet, the head of the Apple software team, they came to a new, better alternative to Objective-C language that was at first named Shiny (as in "this new shiny thing").

More than a year later, Lattner presented this project to his colleagues and managers at Apple. They admired the work Chris had done and designated a team of developers to continue the project.

A lot of new features like Audio Return Channel that were added to Objective-C at that time actually came from Swift, and the team was considering just slowly upgrading Objective-C. However, one of the main features of Swift is its memory safety. And if one takes memory management out of a C-like language, there would not be much C left in it. Therefore, they progressed on a path toward Swift. And at the start, it was not planned as open source. But, on December 3, 2015, the Swift version 2.2 was made open-source under the Apache License 2.0. for Apple's platforms and Linux. A full version history including support for various operating systems goes like this:[1]

Version	Release Date	macOS	Linux	Windows
Swift 1.0	September 9, 2014	Yes	No	No
Swift 1.1	October 22, 2014	Yes	No	No
Swift 1.2	April 8, 2015	Yes	No	No
Swift 2.0	September 21, 2015	Yes	No	No
Swift 2.1	October 20, 2015	Yes	No	No
Swift 2.2	March 21, 2016	Yes	Yes	No
Swift 2.2.1	May 3, 2016	Yes	Yes	No
Swift 3.0	September 13, 2016	Yes	Yes	No
Swift 3.0.1	October 28, 2016	Yes	Yes	No
Swift 3.0.2	December 13, 2016	Yes	Yes	No
Swift 3.1	March 27, 2017	Yes	Yes	No
Swift 3.1.1	April 21, 2017	Yes	Yes	No
Swift 4.0	September 19, 2017	Yes	Yes	No
Swift 4.0.2	November 1, 2017	Yes	Yes	No

(Continued)

---

[1] https://swiftversion.net/, Swift

Version	Release Date	macOS	Linux	Windows
Swift 4.0.3	December 5, 2017	Yes	Yes	No
Swift 4.1	March 29, 2018	Yes	Yes	No
Swift 4.1.1	May 4, 2018	No	Yes	No
Swift 4.1.2	May 31, 2018	Yes	Yes	No
Swift 4.1.3	July 27, 2018	No	Yes	No
Swift 4.2	September 17, 2018	Yes	Yes	No
Swift 4.2.1	October 30, 2018	Yes	Yes	No
Swift 4.2.2	February 4, 2019	No	Yes	No
Swift 4.2.3	February 28, 2019	No	Yes	No
Swift 4.2.4	March 29, 2019	No	Yes	No
Swift 5.0	March 25, 2019	Yes	Yes	No
Swift 5.0.1	April 18, 2019	Yes	Yes	No
Swift 5.0.2	July 15, 2019	No	Yes	No
Swift 5.0.3	August 30, 2019	No	Yes	No
Swift 5.1	September 10, 2019	Yes	Yes	No
Swift 5.1.1	October 11, 2019	No	Yes	No
Swift 5.1.2	November 7, 2019	Yes	Yes	No
Swift 5.1.3	December 13, 2019	Yes	Yes	No
Swift 5.1.4	January 31, 2020	No	Yes	No
Swift 5.1.5	March 9, 2020	No	Yes	No
Swift 5.2	March 24, 2020	Yes	Yes	No
Swift 5.2.1	March 30, 2020	No	Yes	No
Swift 5.2.2	April 15, 2020	Yes	Yes	No
Swift 5.2.3	April 29, 2020	No	Yes	No
Swift 5.2.4	May 20, 2020	Yes	Yes	No
Swift 5.2.5	August 5, 2020	No	Yes	No
Swift 5.3	September 16, 2020	Yes	Yes	Yes
Swift 5.3.1	November 13, 2020	Yes	Yes	Yes
Swift 5.3.2	December 15, 2020	Yes	Yes	Yes
Swift 5.3.3	January 25, 2021	Yes	Yes	Yes
Swift 5.4	April 26, 2021	Yes	Yes	Yes
Swift 5.4.1	May 25, 2021	No	Yes	Yes
Swift 5.4.2	June 28, 2021	Yes	Yes	Yes

Through version 3.0, Swift had experiences certain stability issues. It was frequently modified in backward-incompatible ways, resulting in older tutorials being too outdated to use. In addition, the programs scripted in one version of Swift had problems working together with ones scripted in another version of Swift. This problem was solved when Swift 5 introduced Application Binary Interface (ABI) stability. Overall, at the times when these issues occurred, the core team has expressed that source code compatibility was most important for them at that period of Swift's journey, so obstacles like these would not be a thing anymore. And indeed, Swift is a mature language now and is very well suited for both small and large projects.

Swift Tools

There are a number of Swift-based tools needed to provide a cohesive development experience for the developer's community. Those that are most useful in daily activities include the following:[2]

- **XCODE:** The Xcode Integrated development environment is at the center of the Apple development experience. Closely integrated with the Cocoa and Cocoa Touch frameworks, Xcode is an incredibly productive environment for building apps for Mac, iPhone, iPad, Apple Watch, and Apple TV.

- **SWIFTJSON:** JavaScript Object Notation, or JSON for short, is a common way to transfer data to and from

---

[2] https://www.education-ecosystem.com/guides/programming/swift/history/, Education ecosystem

web services. It is simple to use and human-readable, which is why it is so widely popular. SwiftJSON is the best way to operate with JSON data in Swift.

- **PhoneGap:** PhoneGap is an open-source solution for building cross-platform mobile apps with standards-based Web technologies like HTML, JavaScript, and CSS.

- **GHUNIT:** GHUnit is a test framework for Mac OS X and iOS. It can be used standalone or with other testing frameworks like SenTestingKit or Google Tag Manager.

- **EUREKA:** Eureka is a library to create dynamic table-view forms from a Digital Subscriber Line (DSL) specification in Swift. This DSL basically consists of Rows, Sections and Forms. A Form is a collection of Sections and a Section is a collection of Rows.

- **RX SWIFT:** Rx is a generic abstraction of computation expressed through an Observable interface. Like the original Rx, its intention is to enable easy composition of asynchronous operations and event/data streams.

- **OBJECTMAPPER:** ObjectMapper is a framework written in Swift that makes it easy for you to convert your model objects (classes and structures) to and from JSON.

- **REFACTORATOR:** Refactorator is an Xcode plugin for refactoring Swift and Objective-C code. It will rename public or internal vars, functions, and enums. For private and local entities, it is recommended to use Xcode's existing "Edit All in Scope" functionality.

- **SPRING:** Spring is a library to simplify iOS animations in Swift. It has grown into a full-blown animation library that supports every View, Transitions, Loading Animation and a lot more.

- **IUI:** IUI is a framework consisting of a JavaScript library, CSS, and images for developing advanced mobile website applications.

Right now, Swift is in the nineth place[3] in the Popularity of Programming Language Index, just below its predecessor. It is widely used for development in the Apple ecosystem, and it is quite clear that Apple itself has moved on from Objective-C to Swift as their language of choice for the future.

What is more, Swift engineers are in high demand among technology companies. Application developers are one of the most sought-after professions in the job market, and Swift is the main app programming language for iOS. Because Apple invests heavily in Swift, it will continue to advance it for a long time and promote it to the top of the programming languages.

However, there is also a flip side to that too. The language and its users are much involved in the Apple ecosystem, and its future highly depends on the progression of Apple. Fortunately, the language's open-source nature enables developers to diversify against any potential threats by creating frameworks and applications for Swift outside the Apple ecosystem.

At the same time, it is not very productive to compare Swift to most other modern programming languages.

---

[3] https://pypl.github.io/PYPL.html, PYPL

Nevertheless, Swift does have quite a lot of strong points such as safety and ease of use that makes it as good of a language as other modern programming languages like Java or PHP. Therefore, we may recreate a situation where you are building an application for an Apple product, such as an iOS app. In that case, you have two choices that are not Swift:

- **Objective-C:** Objective-C is a superset of the C programming language with Object-oriented programming capabilities and a dynamic runtime. It used to be the language of choice for Apple products before, and multiple legacy codebases still apply it. Even though it is more popular according to the PYPL index (eighth place) that tracks searches for language tutorials, it is clear that Objective-C is in gradual decline. Most of the things that Objective-C can complete, Swift can do in a more impressive and safer way, so it is not particularly recommended to start most of the new projects in Objective-C.

- **Cross-platform frameworks:** Additionally, there are multiple cross-platform frameworks out there that enable developers to develop for Android and iOS systems at the same time. Among them, we can name React Native, Flutter, and Xamarin. These are a practical choice if you need to quickly launch a simple app on multiple platforms, but they do bring performance costs and can raise some problems if you need non-standard elements for your app that the framework simply does not support. To put it simply, in case you do not really care when deciding on cross-platform versus native, you might end up doing two times the work instead of saving half of it.

Swift as the First Programming Language

Each programming language has its unique characteristics, strengths, and weaknesses. Among Swift's advantages are its practicality and increased developer productivity, letting developers to quickly create prototypes and minimum viable products or MVPs. At the same time, Swift is a suitable tool for building large applications like Twitter or Waze.

Many developers consider Swift to be their first choice for the first programming language. Apple and the Swift community have put a lot of resources and effort into creating easy-to-read materials, high-quality instructive documentation, and a supportive setting for new Swift developers. Therefore, if you are a new developer thinking about which language to start with, following are some arguments in favor of Swift:

- Swift is used for writing programs for a range of Apple devices, so having learned one language, you can work on all of them. And if you are an entrepreneur, creating programs for Apple devices with Swift is guaranteed to give you access to a well-paying audience of Apple Store users.

- Apple is a cutting-edge technology giant, which also means you will always be able to work and experiment with modern tools, features, and libraries.

- If you prefer working as a hired specialist, knowing Swift on an intermediate level increases your future employment opportunities by a lot.

- Swift is relatively easy to learn and you can easily find a large amount of free quality Swift content thanks to the Swift programming language's community.

Swift is a well-designed and well-promoted alternative to the Objective-C language that employs modern programming-language theory concepts and strives to present a simpler syntax. By default, Swift does not display pointers and other unsafe accessors, in contrast to Objective-C, which uses pointers pervasively to refer to object instances.

Additionally, Objective-C's tends to apply Smalltalk-like syntax for making method calls has been replaced with a dot-notation style and namespace system more familiar to programmers from other common object-oriented languages like Java. Swift prefers to introduce true named parameters while retaining key Objective-C concepts, including protocols, closures, and categories, often replacing former syntax with cleaner versions and allowing these concepts to be applied to other language structures, like enumerated types.

Closure Support

Similarly, Swift supports closures also known as lambdas in other languages. To illustrate with an example:[4]

```
// Here is a closure
(arg1: Int, arg2: Int) -> Int in
    return arg1 + arg2
```

---

[4] https://github.com/apple/swift-evolution/blob/b394ae8fff585c8fd-c27a50422ea8a90f13138d2/proposals/0279-multiple-trailing-closures.md, Github

Swift has a trailing closure syntax like this:

```
//This function takes a closure or function
that returns an int and then just evaluates
the function.
func a(closure a: () -> Int) -> Int {
    return a()
}

//Without trailing closure syntax
a(closure: {return 1})

//With trailing closure syntax
a {return 1}
```

String Support

Under the Cocoa and Cocoa Touch environments, many common classes were treated as part of the Foundation Kit library. This included the NSString string library (using Unicode, UTF-8 in Swift 5, changed from UTF-16), the NSArray and NSDictionary collection classes. Objective-C allowed some of these objects to be created on the fly within the language, but once created, the objects were manipulated with object calls. For instance, in Objective-C containing two NSStrings required method calls similar to this:[5]

```
NSString *str = @"hello,";
str = [str stringByAppendingString:@"
world"];
```

---

[5] https://github.com/apple/swift-evolution/blob/b394ae8fff585c8fd-c27a50422ea8a90f13138d2/proposals/0279-multiple-trailing-closures.md, Github

In Swift, many of these basic types have been promoted to the language's core, therefore could be manipulated directly. For instance, strings are invisibly linked to NSString (when Foundation is imported) and can now be grouped with the + operator, allowing greatly simplified syntax; the prior example becoming:

```
var str = "hello,"
str += " world"
```

Access Control

Swift supports five access control levels for symbols: open, public, internal, fileprivate, and private. Unlike many object-oriented languages, these access controls do not follow standard inheritance hierarchies. Resulting in private indicating that a symbol is accessible only in the immediate scope, fileprivate indicating it is accessible only from within the file, internal stating it is accessible within the containing module, public stating it is accessible from any module, and open (only for classes and their methods) indicating that the class may be subclassed outside of the module.

Options and Chaining

An important new feature in Swift is option types. Option types allow references or values to operate in a manner similar to the common pattern in C, where a pointer may refer to a value or may be null. This implies that non-optional types cannot result in a null-pointer error; the compiler can ensure this is not possible.

Optional types are typically created with the Optional mechanism—to make an Integer that is nullable, one would use a declaration similar to var optionalInteger: Optional<Int>.

As in C#, Swift also includes syntactic sugar for this, allowing one to indicate a variable is optional by placing a question mark after the type name, var optionalInteger: Int?. Variables or constants that are marked optional either have a value of the underlying type or are nil. Optional types are referred to as the base type, resulting in a different instance. Thus, String and String? are fundamentally different types, the latter has more in common with Int? than String.

In order to access the value inside, presuming it is not nil, it should be unwrapped to expose the instance inside. This is performed with the! operator in the following manner:[6]

```
let myValue = anOptionalInstance!.
someMethod()
```

In this case, the ! operator unwraps anOptionalInstance to display the instance inside, allowing the method call to be made on it. If anOptionalInstance is nil, a null-pointer error occurs. This can be annoying in practice, so Swift also includes the concept of optional chaining to test whether the instance is nil and then unwrap it if it is non-null:

```
let myValue = anOptionalInstance?.
someMethod()
```

In this case, the runtime calls someMethod only if anOptionalInstance is not nil, suppressing the error. Typically

---

[6] https://github.com/apple/swift-evolution/blob/b394ae8fff585c8fd-c27a50422ea8a90f13138d2/proposals/0279-multiple-trailing-closures.md, Github

this requires the programmer to test whether myValue is nil before proceeding. The origin of the term chaining comes from the more common case where several method calls are chained together. To illustrate with an example:

```
let aTenant = aBuilding.tenantList[5]
let theirLease = aTenant.leaseDetails
let leaseStart = theirLease?.startDate
```

Which can later be reduced to:

```
let leaseStart = aBuilding.tenantList[5].
leaseDetails?.startDate The ? syntax
circumvents the pyramid of doom.
```

At the same time, Swift 2 introduced the new keyword guard for cases in which code should stop executing if some condition is unmet:

```
guard let leaseStart = aBuilding.
TenantList[5]?.leaseDetails?.startDate else
{
    //handle the error case where anything
in the chain is nil
    //else scope must exit the current
method or loop
}
//continue, knowing that leaseStart is not
nil
```

Using this guard has three benefits. While the syntax can act as an if statement, its primary advantage is inferring non-nullability. Where an if statement requires a case, guard assumes the case based on the condition provided. Also, since guard has no scope, with the exception of the else closure, leaseStart is presented as an unwrapped optional to the guard's super-scope. Lastly, if the guard statement's test fails, Swift requires the else to exit the current method or loop, ensuring leaseStart never is accessed when nil. This is achieved with the keywords return, continue, break, or throw, or by calling a function returning a Never or displaying a fatalError().

Objective-C, on the other hand, was weakly typed and allowed any method to be called on any object at any time. If the method call failed, there was a default handler in the runtime that returned nil. That meant that no unwrapping or testing was needed, the equivalent statement in Objective-C:

```
leaseStart = [[[aBuilding tenantList:5]
leaseDetails] startDate]
```

Would return nil, and this could be tested. However, this also demanded that all method calls be dynamic, which results in significant overhead. Swift's use of optionals provides a similar mechanism for testing and dealing with nils but does so in a manner that allows the compiler to use static dispatch because the unwrapping action is called on a defined instance or the wrapper, versus occurring in the runtime dispatch system.

Value Types

In many object-oriented languages, objects are illustrated internally in two parts. The object is stored as a block of data located on the heap, while the name (or "handle") to that object is represented by a pointer. Objects are passed between methods by copying the value of the pointer, allowing the same underlying data on the heap to be accessed by anyone with a copy. In contrast, basic types like integers and floating-point values are represented directly; the handle holds the data, not a pointer to it, and that data is passed directly to methods by copying. These styles of access are termed pass-by-reference in the case of objects, and pass-by-value for basic types.

Nevertheless, both concepts have their advantages and disadvantages. Objects are useful if you are dealing with data that is large, like the description of a window or the contents of a document. In these cases, access to that data is provided by copying a 32- or 64-bit value, versus copying an entire data structure. However, smaller values like integers are the same size as pointers (typically both are one word), so there is no advantage to passing a pointer, versus passing the value. Also, pass-by-reference inherently requires an additional dereferencing operation, which can result in noticeable overhead in some operations, typically those used with these basic value types, like mathematics.

Similar to C# but in contrast to most other object-oriented languages, Swift offers built-in support for objects using either pass-by-reference or pass-by-value semantics, the former using the class declaration and the latter using struct. In Swift, structs have almost all the same features as classes: methods, implementing protocols, and using the extension mechanisms. For this reason, Apple terms all data generically as instances, versus objects or values. Yet keep in mind that structs do not support inheritance hierarchies.

As a programmer, you are free to choose which semantics are more suitable for each data structure in the application. Larger structures like windows would be defined as classes, allowing them to be passed around as pointers. Smaller structures, like a 2D point, can be identified as structs, which will be pass-by-value and allow direct access to their internal data with no dereference. The performance improvement inherent to the pass-by-value concept is such that Swift applies these types for almost all common data types, including Int and Double, and types normally represented by objects, like String and Array. Using value types can result in significant performance improvements in user applications as well.

In order to make sure that even the largest structs do not cause a performance penalty when they are handed off, Swift applies copy on write so that the objects are copied only if and when the program attempts to change a value in them. This basically means that the various accessors have what is in effect a pointer to the same data storage. So when the data is physically stored as one instance in memory, at the level of the application, these values are independent and physical separation is enforced by copy on write only if necessary.

Protocol-Oriented Programming

It is a well-known fact that the basic concepts of Swift are similar to Objective-C at its core. A key feature of Objective-C is its support for categories, methods that can be included to extend classes at runtime. Categories let extending classes in place to insert new functions with no need to subclass or even have access to the original source code. An example might be to add spell checker support to the base NSString class, which means all instances of NSString in the application gain spell checking. The system is also widely applied as an organizational technique, allowing related code to be gathered into library-like extensions. Swift continues to support this concept, although they are now termed extensions, and declared with the keyword extension. But unlike Objective-C, Swift can also add new properties accessors, types, and enums to extant instances.

Another key feature of Objective-C that is worth mentioning (in relation to Swift) is its use of protocols, known in most modern languages as interfaces. Protocols are inserted to guarantee that a particular class implements a set of methods, meaning that other objects in the system can call those methods on any object supporting that protocol. This is often used in modern object-oriented languages as a substitute for multiple inheritances, although the feature sets are not entirely similar. A common example of a protocol in Cocoa is the NSCopying protocol, which uses one method, copyWithZone, that executes deep copying on objects.

In Objective-C, and most other languages implementing the protocol concept, it is up to the programmer to ensure that the required methods are implemented in each class. Swift adds the ability to insert these methods using extensions and to use generic programming to activate them. Combined, these allow protocols to be scripted once and support a wide variety of instances. Also, the extension mechanism can be used to include protocol conformance to an object that does not list that protocol in its definition. For instance, a protocol could be declared called StringConvertible, which ensures that instances that relate to the protocol implement a toString method that returns a String. In Swift, this can be declared with code like this:[7]

```
protocol StringConvertible
{
    func toString() -> String
}
```

This protocol can now be included to String, with no access to the base class's source:

```
extension String: StringConvertible
{
    func toString() -> String
    {
        self
    }
}
```

In Swift, like many modern languages supporting inter-faces, protocols can be used as types, which means variables and methods can be defined by protocol instead of their specific type:

```
var someSortOfPrintableObject:
StringConvertible
print(someSortOfPrintableObject.toString())
```

---

[7] https://developer.apple.com/documentation/foundation/nscopying, Apple

It does not matter what sort of instance someSortOfPrintableObject is, the compiler will ensure that it conforms to the protocol and thus this code is secure. This syntax also means that collections can be based on protocols also, like let printableArray = [StringConvertible].

As Swift processes structs and classes as similar concepts, both extensions and protocols are extensively utilized in Swift's runtime to provide a rich Application Programming Interface (API) based on structs. For example, Swift uses an extension to activate the Equatable protocol to many of their basic types, like Strings and Arrays, allowing them to be compared with the == operator. A simple example of how all of these features interact can be seen in the concept of default protocol implementations:

```
func !=<T: Equatable>(LHS: T, rhs: T) ->
Bool
```

This function determines a method that is suited to any instance conforming to Equatable, providing a not equals function. Any instance, class or struct, automatically gains this implementation simply by conforming to Equatable. As many instances gain Equatable through their base implementations or other generic extensions, most basic objects in the runtime gain equals and not equals with no code.

This combination of protocols, defaults, protocol inheritance, and extensions allows many of the functions normally connected to classes and inheritance to be implemented on value types. Correctly applied, this can lead to dramatic performance advancements with no significant limits in API. This concept is so widely utilized within Swift that Apple has begun calling it a protocol-oriented programming language. Moreover, they recommend addressing many of the problem domains normally solved through classes and inheritance using protocols and structs instead.

Libraries, Runtime, and Development

On Apple systems, Swift uses the same runtime as the extant Objective-C system, but requires iOS 7 or macOS 10.9 or higher. It also depends on Grand Central Dispatch. Normally, Swift and Objective-C code can be used in one program, and by extension, C and C++ also. However, in contrast to C, C++ code cannot be used directly from Swift. An Objective-C or C wrapper should be created between Swift and C++. In the case of Objective-C, Swift has considerable access to the object model and can be used to subclass, extend and use Objective-C code to provide protocol support. Yet the converse is not possible: Swift class cannot be subclassed in Objective-C.

In order to assist the development of such programs, and enable re-using of extant code, Xcode 6 and higher offers a semi-automated system that builds and maintains a bridging header to expose Objective-C code to Swift. This takes the shape of an additional header file that simply defines or imports all of the Objective-C symbols that are requested by the project's Swift code. At that point, Swift can refer to the types, functions, and variables declared in those imports as though they were written in Swift.

Objective-C code can also apply Swift code directly, by importing an automatically maintained header file with Objective-C declarations of the project's Swift symbols. For instance, an Objective-C file in a mixed project called "MyApp" could access Swift classes or functions with the code #import "MyApp-Swift.h." However, not all symbols are available through this mechanism, but you can use all of the Swift-specific features like generic types, non-object optional types, sophisticated enums, or even Unicode identifiers that can render a symbol inaccessible from Objective-C.

Swift also has limited support for attributes, metadata that is produced by the development environment and is not necessarily part of the compiled code. Like Objective-C, attributes use the @ syntax, but the currently available set is small. One example is the @IBOutlet attribute, which symbolizes a given value in the code as an outlet, available for use within Interface Builder (IB). An outlet is a device that binds the value of the on-screen display to an object in code.

On non-Apple systems, Swift does not rely on an Objective-C runtime or other Apple system libraries; a set of Swift "Corelib" implementations replace them. These include a "swift-core-libs-foundation" to stand in for the Foundation Kit, a "swift-core-libs-libdispatch" to stand in for the Grand Central Dispatch, and a "swift-core-libs-xctest" instead of the XCTest APIs from Xcode.

In addition, as of Xcode 13.x, Apple has also added a major new user interface (UI) paradigm called SwiftUI.

SwiftUI was created to replace the older IB paradigm with a new declarative development paradigm.

Memory Management

When it comes to managing memory, Swift uses the Automatic Reference Counting (ARC) tool. Prior to introducing ARC in 2011 to allow for easier memory allocation and deallocation, Apple used to require Objective-C manual memory management. However, there is one problem with ARC, which is the possibility of creating a strong reference cycle, where objects reference each other in a way that you can reach the object you started from by following references (as in, A references B, B references A). This causes them to become leaked into memory as they are never released. Swift provides the keywords weak and unowned to prevent strong reference cycles. Usually, a parent-child relationship would use a strong reference while a child-parent would use either weak reference, where parents and children can be unrelated, or unowned where a child always has a parent, but parent may not have a child. Weak references must be optional variables since they can change and become nil.

Additionally, a closure within a class can also create a strong reference cycle by capturing self-references. And self-references to be treated as weak or unowned can be indicated using a capture list.

Debugging and Other Elements

A key element of the Swift system is its ability to be cleanly debugged and run within the development environment, using a read–eval–print loop (REPL), giving it interactive properties more in common with the scripting abilities of Python than traditional system programming languages. The REPL will be discussed in detail in the following chapter. But basically, these are interactive views running within the Xcode environment that respond to code or debugger changes on-the-fly. Playgrounds allow programmers to include Swift code along with markdown documentation. If some code changes over time or with regard to some other ranged input value, the view can be used with the Timeline Assistant to display the output in an animated way. In addition, Xcode has debugging features for Swift development including breakpoints, step through and step over statements, as well as UI element placement breakdowns for app developers.

Performance

Many of the Swift features introduced so far have well-known performance and safety trade-offs. Apple has implemented multiple optimizations methods in order to reduce this overhead. Yet when it comes to analyzing Swift performance, there is no better way to do it than run a comparison check in relation to other languages. Thus, since Swift is considered a C family programming language, let's see in which ways it is similar to it:

- Most C operators are used in Swift, but there are some new operators, for example, to support integer operations with overflow.

- Curly braces are similarly used to group statements.

- Variables are assigned using an equals sign, but compared using two consecutive equals signs. A new identity operator, ===, is provided to check if two data elements refer to the same object.

- Square brackets are used with arrays, both to declare them and to get a value at a given index in one of them.

It also has multiple similarities to Objective-C:

- Runs basic numeric types (Int, UInt, Float, Double).

- Class methods are inherited, like instance methods; self-in-class methods is the class the method was called on.

- Similar operations of the enumeration syntax.

However, major differences from Objective-C include the following:

- Statements do not need to end with semicolons (;), though these must be used to allow more than one statement on a line.

- No header files.

- Uses type inference.

- Functions are treated as first-class objects.

- Enumeration cases can have associated data (algebraic data types).

- Operators can be redefined for classes (operator overloading), and new operators can be defined.

- Strings fully support Unicode. Most Unicode characters can be used in either identifiers or operators.

- No exception handling. Swift 2 introduced a different and incompatible error-handling model.

- Pointers are not exposed by default. There is no need for the programmer to keep track of and mark names for referencing or dereferencing.

- No need to use break statements in switch blocks. Individual cases do not fall through to the next case unless the fall-through statement is used.

- Variables and constants are always initialized, and array bounds are always checked.

- Integer overflows, which result in undefined behavior for signed integers in C, are trapped as a run-time error in Swift. Programmers can choose to allow overflows by using the special arithmetical operators &+, &-, &*, &/, and &%. The properties min and max are defined in Swift for all integer types and can be used to safely check for potential overflows, versus relying on constants defined for each type in external libraries.

- The pre- and post-increment and decrement operators (i++, --i) are unsupported from Swift 3 onward.

TECHNICAL REQUIREMENTS

Swift is known for its straightforward operating mode. And there are not that many technical requirements you need to think about prior to starting up. Mainly, only if you wish to make use of Swift's hardware-accelerated solver capabilities you would need to install a graphics card and driver supporting OpenCL 1.1 or later. It is strongly recommended that you have a dedicated graphics card rather than rely on graphics capabilities offered by on-motherboard chips from Intel. However, if you do rely on integrated graphics, please ensure you are using the latest stable driver available. Alternatively, if graphics hardware is not available on your system, the AMD OpenCL SDK (version 2.9.1 is recommended) can provide a software driver that will let you operate Swift in a central processing unit (CPU)-only manner.

In addition that, there are also a few standard operating system requirements that you might want to note:

- **Windows:** Swift Windows packages are suitable for Windows XP, Windows 7, or Windows 8. It is recommended that you uninstall the previous version of the software before installing the new version, and in order to install Swift on Windows, simply run the installation executable and follow the on-screen prompts.

- **Mac:** Swift is currently supported on Mac OSX 10.7-9 (Lion, Mountain Lion, and Mavericks). Support for previous versions of OSX as well as the new Yosemite will be provided in the near future. The installation procedure is quite simple—open the. dmg file, run the installation package inside and follow the on-screen prompts. Swift will then be accessible from within the Applications folder.

- **Linux:** All Linux packages are built for LSB 4.1 compliant RPM-based systems, the most common of which include SLED13, RHEL, and Ubuntu 13.04. To install the packages, make sure the LSB-4.1 packages are installed as well, and then you can activate Swift by using the command (sudo access may be required):

```
rpm -Ivh <swift package name>.rpm
```

Swift will then be placed to the/opt/csiro.au/Swift-gui-fsp directory.

For older systems that pre-date LSB 4.1, installation of the RPMs will have to require using the –nodeps option or its equivalent due to the dependency on "lsb>=4.1". This dependency is there to assist package management systems install the packages on which Swift depends. When installing on older systems with the –nodeps option, you are strongly advised to install the most recent lsb package that your version supports.

- **Installing on Debian-based Systems:** In order to install Swift on Debian-based systems, you will first need to convert the RPM packages into the. deb format using alien. Keep in mind that certain options must be used to preserve the pre/post-install/uninstall scripts and to prevent the release number from being incremented. Failure to do this can result in issues with misleading error messages. The recommended syntax to use is the following:

```
sudo alien -kcv --bump=0 <swift package
name>.rpm
```

INSTALLATION OF SWIFT

In order to download the installer and its components, please use this link to access the official Swift website—https://swift.org/download/#releases

After completing a standard set of instructions, the installation of swift would be completed. Then you should launch the Xcode and choose the toolchain option to select Swift development language:[8]

- **For macOS:** The default location for the toolchain on Mac where it can be installed is through the terminal with the following command:

  ```
  $export TOOLCHAINS=swift
  ```

- **For Linux:** If you installed the Swift toolchain on Linux to a directory other than the system root, you

---

[8] https://swift.org/getting-started/, Swift

will need to run the following command, using the actual path of your Swift installation:

```
$ export PATH=/path/to/Swift/usr/
bin:"${PATH}"
```

- **For Windows:** You will need to install both the tool-chain installer from the main Swift Download page and certain components from Visual Studio 2019—https://visualstudio.microsoft.com/

The following Visual Studio components are required:

1. **MSVC v142:** VS 2019 C++ x64/x86 build tools (v14.25)1 Microsoft Visual Studio Component VC.Tools.x86.x64

2. **Windows Universal C Runtime:** Microsoft Visual Studio Component Windows 10SDK

3. **Windows 10 SDK (10.0.17763.0)2:** Microsoft Visual Studio Component Windows 10SDK.17763

The following additional Visual Studio components are also recommended:

1. **C++ CMake tools for Windows:** Microsoft Visual Studio Component VC.CMake.Project

2. **Git for Windows:** Microsoft Visual Studio Component Git

3. **Python 3 64-bit (3.7.8):** Component CPython.x64

The default installation location for the toolchain on Windows is %SystemDrive%\Library\Developer\Toolchains.

Once you are all-set, the first Swift-specific features you shall face and work with would be the following:

- Advanced control flow

- Fast and concise iteration over range or collection

- Functional programming patterns

- Multiple return values and tuples

- In-built error handling

- Closures unified and function pointer

- Structs that support method, protocols, and extensions

The other feature that is overarching the above list would be safety. Swift was originally designed to be safer than other languages and to eliminate the other unsafe code. It helps in managing the memory automatically and making it easy to define the intent. Another important feature is that swift objects cannot be nil; otherwise, it throws a compile-time error. Due to that, your coding would be easier, cleaner, and safer without any run time crashes.

As the Swift code is easily available on Github, it is being maintained by the larger support community of swift developers that are dedicated to increasing the performance of the language, and since Swift is open to any platform, it can be ported across a wide range of platforms and devices.

In addition, Swift fully supports strings with Unicode. It basically means that the enumeration classes can have data associated with it, and the new operators can be defined for the classes, or operators can be redefined. There is no need to use the break statement in switch blocks as the variables and constants are always initialized and checked the bound arrays.

Swift is developed to replace the Objective-C language and C language. Therefore, its applications are getting loaded at a faster rate. Additionally, Swift code is more expressive and easy to read and use. The modern features that it offers are easy to learn. And overall, Swift is getting better and better over the years with its latest versions.

In this chapter, you learned how to install and get your development environment ready for operating with Swift. We also showed you how Swift can be comparable to other languages in terms of performance for most of the tasks. You should now have the foundation required to be able to review and analyze basic Swift syntax building, running programs on C++ as well as learning how to use various data types like Strings, Ints, Floats, and Bools.

CHAPTER 2

Getting Started with Swift

IN THIS CHAPTER

➤ Reviewing basic Swift syntax

➤ Learning how to use various data types

➤ Building and Running Programs on C++

In the previous chapter, we learned about the history of the Swift programming language, its main characteristics, and advantages. This chapter shall walk you through installing and setting up your development environment so you can follow further instructions and examples in this book. First, we shall look at the Basic Swift Language Syntax and then review various data types such as Strings, Ints, Floats, and Bools. Additionally, you are going to learn more about

DOI: 10.1201/9781003254089-2

running Programs on C++ and using the read–eval–print loop (REPL) tool.

BASIC SWIFT LANGUAGE SYNTAX

Like many modern programming languages, Swift draws its most basic syntax from the programming language C. Therefore, in case you have previous programming experience in other C-inspired languages, many aspects of Swift will seem familiar, for example:

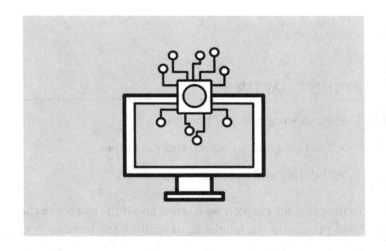

- Programs are made up of statements, executed sequentially.

- More than one statement is allowed per editor line when separated by a semicolon (;).

- Units of work in Swift are modularized using functions and organized into types.

- Functions accept one or more parameters and return values.

- Single and multiline comments follow the same syntax as in C++ and Java.

- Swift data type names and usage are similar to that in Java, C#, and C++.

- Swift has the concept of named variables, which are mutable, and named constants, which are immutable.

- Swift has both struct and class semantics, as do C++ and C#.

At the same time, Swift has some improvements and differences from C-inspired languages that you may have to get accustomed to. For instance, semicolons are not inserted at the end of statements—except when used to separate multiple statements typed on the same line in a source file. Swift has no main() method to act as the program's starting point when the operating system loads the application. General programs begin at the first line of code of the program's source file—as is the case in most interpreted languages. Also, functions in Swift place the function return type at the right-hand side of the function declaration, rather than the left. And function parameter declaration syntax is mostly inspired by Objective-C, which is quite different and at times confusing for Java, C#, and C++ developers. In addition, the difference between a struct and a class in Swift is similar to what we have in C# (value type versus reference type), but not the same as in C++ (both are the same, except struct members are public by default).

In order to start making iOS apps, you need to download a program called Xcode from the Mac App Store. Xcode is mostly known as an integrated development environment or IDE for short. In general terms, an IDE is simply a program that provides you with the necessary tools to write a piece of software. Xcode in particular helps you run and test Swift code on your computer. Xcode and Swift are both software development products developed by Apple. And even though you utilize both products to develop Apple-based applications, they play different roles in the development process.

As mentioned, Xcode is an IDE developed by Apple that allows you to build apps for iOS, macOS, tvOS, and watchOS. Launched in 2003, Xcode continues to progress. Since version 5.x in 2013, Apple has consistently released a new version on an annual basis. As Apple launched new products such as the iPad, iPhone, Apple TV, and Apple Watch, they included development support into the Xcode IDE platform. Moreover, Xcode comes with a range of features you would expect in an enterprise IDE such as:

- **Language Support:** The Xcode IDE supports the Swift programming language and offers developers the flexibility to write code in C, C++, Objective-C, Objective-C++, Java, Applescript, Python, and Ruby.

- **Output Capability:** Xcode builds large binary files. It is capable of including code for various architectures that conform to the Mach-0 format. As these are universal binary files, it allows the application to operate on PowerPC as well as 32-bit and 64-bit Intel x86 platforms.

- **Debugging and Compiling:** When you need to build apps for ARM, you can leverage specialist components like the iOS software development kit (SDK). This feature makes it possible to compile and debug applications that need to run on iOS and the new Apple M1 chipset.

- **SwiftUI:** Xcode's SwiftUI allows developers to design user interfaces for all Apple platforms leveraging the Swift programming language. It has automatic support for modern user's interface additional features such as dynamic type, dark mode, localization, and accessibility.

In addition to the above-mentioned coding features, Xcode offers developers a range of functionality to advance their workflow and streamline the software development process. To illustrate, version 12 of Xcode comes with document tabs that allow you to alter the navigator font sizes and offers enhanced code completion. A great usability feature sorely missed in previous versions. Moreover, since Xcode 12 is also universal app-ready, it lets you test a single code base across multiple architectures. Taking the family of Apple operating systems into account, it also comes with built-in multiplatform app templates. This feature allows you to work on new projects and share code among macOS, iOS, watchOS, and tvOS using SwiftUI and the lifecycle APIs.

Just to clarify, Xcode and Swift, being two Apple technologies, do not need to compete. Instead, they complement each other and are the preferred platform to develop apps for macOS, iOS, tvOS, and watchOS. Since Swift is open source and cross-platform, developers can apply

Xcode features to build Linux and Windows apps in addition to applications for Apple devices.

Furthermore, if your primary device is a Mac, developing Swift and Xcode gives you the capability to develop apps for many use cases. Nevertheless, even though these two technologies operate seamlessly together, you do have other choices. As Xcode supports a wide range of programming languages such as C, C++, Java, and Python, you can build apps using these platforms. Yet the real power of integration will still come from using the two Apple technologies together. That is why the Xcode and Swift combination may well be considered as one of the most popular software development platforms.

To continue with the development side, we shall presume you already have an account on the Apple Developer website. Once you are logged in, download Xcode and drop the Xcode icon into the Application folder by simply following the given instructions.

When have XCode installed on your machine, select the Get started with a playground option and enter a name for playground, and select iOS as platform. Following is the code taken from the default Swift Playground Window:

```
import UIKit
var str = "Hello, playground"
```

If you create the same program for the OS X program, then it will include import Cocoa and the program will look like as follows:

```
import Cocoa
var str = "Hello, playground"
```

When the above program gets loaded, it should display the following result in the Playground result area:

```
Hello, playground
```

With that, you can be certain that your Swift programming environment is now ready for work.

Different Elements of the Playground

The most important elements of the playground that you need to focus on for now are the following:

1. **Code editor:** this is where you are going to be typing your Swift code.

2. **Line numbers:** features that will help you refer to different lines of code.

    If you do not have line numbers and want to enable them, just go to Xcode > Preferences > Text Editing > Line Numbers and turn those line numbers on or off.

3. **Status bar:** an area that displays the current status of the playground.

    If the status says that it is ready for you, it only means that Xcode is ready to accept your code and run it.

4. **Show/Hide debug:** allows you to hide or show the debug or console area: the place where you can test your Swift code.

5. **Execute playground:** area that runs all the code in your playground

    Here, you are presented with two options: "Automatically Run" and "Manually Run."

Swift Playground Automatic or Manual Execution

The "Manually Run" mode means you need to click either click this play button or the blue play icon to run your code. Otherwise, setting it to "Automatically Run" means Xcode will automatically activate your playground and update the results every time you edit the code.

The automatic mode is not completely error-free. Sometimes Xcode will not update the results when it is constantly running your playground. If this happens, just click the stop button and hold down the play button to change it to "Manually Run." When the status bar says "Ready," you will be able to click and run your code again.

We have already seen a piece of the Swift program when setting up the initial environment. Let us start once again with the following Hello, World! program created for OS X playground, which includes the following import Cocoa:

```
/* My first program in Swift */
var myString = "Hello, World!"
print(myString)
```

If you create the same program for the iOS playground, then it will include import UIKit, and the program will look as follows:

```
import UIKit
var myString = "Hello, World!"
print(myString)
```

When you run the above program using an appropriate playground, you will get the following result:

```
Hello, World!
```

Let us now see the basic structure of a Swift program, so that it will be easier for you to navigate the basic building blocks of the Swift programming language.

Import in Swift

You can insert the import statement to import any Objective-C framework (or C library) directly into your Swift. To illustrate, the above import cocoa statement makes all Cocoa libraries, APIs, and runtimes that form the development layer for all of OS X, available in Swift.

Worth noting that since Cocoa is implemented in Objective-C, which is a superset of C, it could be easy to mix C and even C++ into your Swift applications.

Tokens in Swift

A Swift program consists of various tokens and a token stands for either a keyword, an identifier, a constant, a string literal, or a symbol. To demonstrate, the following Swift statement consists of three tokens:

```
print("test!")
The individual tokens are:
print("test!")
```

Comments

Comments are like helping passages in your Swift program. They are typically emitted by the compiler. Multi-line comments start with /* and terminate with the characters */ as illustrated here:

```
/* My first program in Swift */
```

Additionally, multi-line comments can be nested in Swift as well. Following is a valid comment in Swift:

```
/* My first program in Swift is Hello, World!
/* Where as second program is Hello, Swift!
*/ */
```

While single-line comments are written using // at the beginning of the comment.

```
//My first program in Swift
```

Semicolons

As stated earlier, Swift does not require you to type a semicolon (;) after each statement in your code, though it is optional. And shall you insert a semicolon, then the compiler will not complain about it.

However, if you are using multiple statements in the same line, then it is required to use a semicolon as a delimiter, otherwise, the compiler will deliver a syntax error. You can write the above Hello, World! program in the following manner:

```
/* My first program in Swift */
var myString = "Hello, World!";
print(myString)
```

Identifiers

A Swift identifier is a term used to identify a variable, function, or any other user-defined component. An identifier typically starts with an alphabet A to Z or a to z or an underscore _ followed by zero or more letters, underscores, and digits (0–9).

Swift does not include special characters such as @, $, and % within identifiers. And since Swift is considered a case-sensitive programming language, Extension and extension are two different identifiers in Swift. Here are some general examples of acceptable identifiers:[1]

-Azad	-zara	-abc	-move_name	-a_123
-myname50	-_temp	-j	-a23b9	-retVal

In order to insert a reserved word as an identifier, you will need to put a backtick (`) before and after it. For instance, the class will not be considered as a valid identifier, but `class` would be treated as valid.

Keywords

The following are the keywords reserved in Swift. These reserved words may not be utilized as constants or variables or any other identifier names, unless they are escaped with backticks:[2]

Keywords used in declarations:

-Class	-deinit	-Enum	-extension
-Func	-import	-Init	-internal
-Let	-operator	-private	-protocol
-public	-static	-struct	-subscript
-typealias	-var		

---

[1] https://www.tutorialspoint.com/swift/swift_basic_syntax.htm, Tutorialspoint

[2] https://www.tutorialspoint.com/swift/swift_basic_syntax.htm, Tutorialspoint

Keywords used in statements:

-break	-case	-continue	-default
-do	-else	-fallthrough	-for
-if	-in	-return	-switch
-where	-while		

Keywords used in expressions and types:

-as	-dynamicType	-false	-is
-nil	-self	-Self	-super
-true	-_COLUMN_	-_FILE_	-_FUNCTION_
-_LINE_			

Keywords used in particular contexts:

-associativity	-convenience	-dynamic	-didSet
-final	-get	-infix	-inout
-lazy	-left	-mutating	-none
-nonmutating	-optional	-override	-postfix
-precedence	-prefix	-Protocol	-required
-right	-set	-Type	-unowned
-weak	-willSet		

Whitespaces

A line containing only whitespace, possibly with a comment, is known as a blank line, and a Swift compiler simply does not see it. Whitespace is the term used in Swift to describe blanks, tabs, newline characters, and comments. Whitespaces separate one part of a statement from another and enable the compiler to recognize where one element in a statement, such as int, ends and the next element begins.

Therefore, in the following statement—var age, there must be at least one whitespace character (usually a space) between var and age for the compiler to be able to identify them. On the other hand, in the following statement:

int fruit = apples + bananas   //get the total fruits

No whitespace characters are needed between fruit and =, or between = and apples, although you are free to include some for better comprehensibility. In addition, space on both sides of operator should be equal, for example:

int fruit = apples +bananas   //is a wrong statement

int fruit = apples + bananas   //is a correct statement

Literals

A literal stands for the source code representation of a value of an integer, floating-point number, or string type. The following are examples of literals:

92   // Integer literal

4.24159   // Floating-point literal

"Hello, World!" // String literal

In case you want to print any data in swift, just use the "print" keyword. The print has three following properties:

Items—items to be printed

Separator—separator between items

Terminator—the value with which line should end.

USING STRINGS, INTS, FLOATS, AND BOOLS

While doing programming in any programming language, you need to know different types of variables to store information. Variables could be described as reserved memory locations where you could store values. This means that when you create a variable, you reserve some space in memory. Based on the data type of a variable, the operating system allocates memory and determines what can be stored in the reserved memory.

Swift offers the programmer a rich assortment of built-in as well as user-defined data types. The collection of built-in data types includes string, integer, floating-point numbers, and Booleans. These data types are also found in most programming languages. In this section, we will discuss each of these most frequently applied data types in detail.

1. **Int or UInt:** An integer data type is used to represent a whole number with no fractional component. More specifically, you can use Int32, Int64 to define 32- or 64-bit signed integer, whereas UInt32 or UInt64 to define 32 or 64 bit unsigned integer variables. You can use the Int keyword to create integer-type variables. For example:

```
// create integer type variable
var number: Int = 3
print(number)
// Output: 3
```

In the above example, we have created an Int type variable named number and assigned 3 to the number.

At the same time, some of the basic properties of integers in swift programming are the following:[3]

Size: Depends on the platform type
Range: -231 to 231-1 (32 bit platform)
-263 to 263-1 (64-bit platform)

Additional points related to Integer types include the following:

- On a 32-bit platform, Int is the same size as Int32.

- On a 64-bit platform, Int is the same size as Int64.

- On a 32-bit platform, UInt is the same size as UInt32.

- On a 64-bit platform, UInt is the same size as UInt64.

To note, Int8, Int16, Int32, and Int64 can also be used to represent 8-Bit, 16-Bit, 32-Bit, and 64-Bit forms of signed integer.

2. **Float:** A float data type represents a number with a fractional component 32-bit, floating-point number, and numbers with smaller decimal points like 3.14159, 0.1, or -273.158. Similarly, you can use the Float keyword to create float-type variables. To illustrate:

```
// create float type variable
let piValue: Float = 3.14
print(value)
// Output: 3.14
```

[3] https://www.programiz.com/swift-programming/data-types, Programiz

In the above example, we have created a Float type variable named piValue and assigned 3.14 point to piValue.

Some of the basic properties of float in swift programming include the following:

Size: 32-bit floating-point number
Range: 1.2×10^{-38} to 3.4×10^{38} (Up to 6 decimal places)

3. **Double:** Like Float, a double data type is also used to represent a number with fractional components, 64-bit floating-point number and at instances when floating-point values are too large. For example, 3.14159, 0.1, or –273.158.

At the same time, Double supports data only up to 15 decimal places, or you can also use the Double keyword to create double variables. To illustrate:

```
// create double type variable
let latitude: Double = 27.7007697012432
print(latitude)
// Output: 27.7007697012432
```

In the above example, we have created a Double type variable named latitude and assigned 27.7007697012432 points to it.

Some of the standard properties of double in swift programming include the following:

Size: 64-bit floating-point number
Range: 2.3×10^{-308} to 1.7×10^{308} (Up to 15 decimal places)

It is also worth mentioning that in case you have a number like 27.7007697012432, you can use either

Double to store the number with more precision (up to 15 decimal places) or Float to store the number with less precision (up to 6 decimal places).

4. **Bool:** This data type represents a Boolean value which is either true or false. A boolean type is generally used to represent logical entities. You should use the Bool keyword to create boolean-type variables. To demonstrate with an example:

```
// create boolean type variable
let passCheck: Bool = true
print(passCheck)

let failCheck: Bool = false
print(failCheck)
```

5. **String:** The string could be described as an ordered collection of characters. For example, "Hello, World!"

The string data type is mostly used to represent textual data. While the String keyword is applied to create string-type variables. For instance:

```
// create string type variable
var language: String = "swift"
print(name)
// Output: swift
```

In the above example, we have created a String type variable named language and assigned a "swift" variable to it.

6. **Character:** This is a single-character string literal. The character data type is mostly used to represent

a single-character string. You can apply the Character keyword to create character-type variables. For example:

```
// create character type variable
var letter: Character = "s"
print(letter)
// Output: s
```

In the above example, we have created a Character type variable named letter and assigned the "s" variable to it. However, if you try to assign more than one character like "ABC" to variables of Character type, you will most likely get an error message.

7. **Optional:** This data type represents a variable that can hold either a value or no value.

8. **Tuples:** The tuples data type is used to combine multiple values in a single Compound Value.

Bound Values

The following list displays the variable type, how much bit width memory it takes to store the value in memory, and what is the maximum and minimum value which can be stored in such types of variables:[4]

Type	Bit Width	Typical Range
(1) Int8	1 byte	−127 to 127
(2) UInt8	1 byte	0 to 255
(3) Int32	4 bytes	−2147483648 to 2147483647
(4) UInt32	4 bytes	0 to 4294967295

---

[4] https://www.tutorialspoint.com/swift/swift_data_types.htm, Tutorialspoint

Type	Bit Width	Typical Range
(5) Int64	8 bytes	−9223372036854775808 to 9223372036854775807
(6) UInt64	8 bytes	0 to 18446744073709551615
(7) Float	4 bytes	1.2E–38 to 3.4E+38 (~6 digits)
(8) Double	8 bytes	2.3E–308 to 1.7E+308 (~15 digits)

Type Aliases

In swift, by using typealiases keyword, you can create a new name for an existing type. The typealiases are helpful whenever you want to create a meaningful name for our existing types. Following is the basic syntax of making up an alternative name to the existing type using typealias keyword:

```
typealias newname = type
```

In addition, the following line instructs the compiler that Feet is another name for Int:

```
typealias Feet = Int
```

With that, the following declaration is perfectly valid and creates an integer variable called distance:

```
typealias Feet = Int
var distance: Feet = 100
print(distance)
```

Now if you run the above program using playground, you will get the following result:

100

Type Safety

Swift is a type-safe programming language that means once we determine a variable with one data type, then it is not possible to assign another data type value to it. As Swift is type-safe, it performs automatic type-checks when compiling your code and marks any mismatched types as errors. To demonstrate with an example:

```
var varA = 32
varA = "This is hello"
print(varA)
```

When you compile the above program, it will produce the following compile-time error:

```
main.swift:2:8: error: cannot assign value
of type 'String' to type 'Int'
varA = "This is hello"
```

Type Inference

In Swift Type inference allows a compiler to automatically deduce the type of a particular expression simply by examining the values you provide. Following is the simple example to deduce the variable value, when the compiler found that it adds the floating values to an integer:

```
var varA = 53453
print(varA)
var varB = 53453.453453
print(varB)
var varC = 53 + 0.45353
print(varC)
```

When you run above program you will get output like this:

53453

53453.453453

53.45353

Creating a String

It is possible to create a String either by using a string literal or by creating an instance of a String class in the following way:[5]

```
// String creation using String literal
var string = "Hello, Swift 4!"
print (string)

// String creation using String instance
var stringB = String("Hello, Swift 4!")
print (stringB)

//Multiple line string

let stringC = """
Hey this is a
example of multiple Line
string
"""

print(stringC)
```

---

[5] https://www.tutorialspoint.com/swift/swift_strings.htm, Tutorialspoint

When the above code is compiled and executed, it produces the following output:

```
Hello, Swift 4!
Hello, Swift 4!
Hey this is a
example of multiple Line
string
```

Empty String

You can create an empty String either by using an empty string literal or creating an instance of String class as illustrated here. You can also check whether a string is empty or not using the Boolean property is Empty.

```
// Empty string creation using String
literal
var stringA = ""

if stringA.isEmpty {
   print ("stringA is empty")
} else {
   print ("stringA is not empty")
}

// Empty string creation using String
instance
let stringB = String()

if stringB.isEmpty {
   print ("stringB is empty")
} else {
   print ("stringB is not empty")
}
```

When the above code is compiled and executed, it displays the following output:

```
stringA is empty
stringB is empty
```

String Constants

You can set whether your String can be modified (or edited) by assigning it to a variable, or it will be constant by assigning it to a constant using let keyword as shown below:

```
// stringA can be modified
var string = "Hello, Swift 4!"
stringA + = "--Readers--"
print(string)

// stringB can not be modified
let stringB = String("Hello, Swift 4!")
stringB + = "--Readers--"
print(stringB)
```

When the above code is combined and implemented, it produces the following result:

```
Playground execution failed: error:
<EXPR>:10:1: error: 'String' is not
convertible to '@lvalue UInt8'
stringB + = "--Readers--"
```

String Interpolation

String interpolation is a way to create a new String value from a mix of constants, variables, literals, and expressions by inserting their values inside a string literal. Each component (variable or constant) that you insert into the string literal is wrapped in a pair of parentheses, prefixed by a backslash. To illustrate with a simple example:

```
var varA = 20
let constA = 100
var varC:Float = 20.0

var stringA = "\(varA) times\(constA) is
equal to\(varC * 100)"
print (stringA)
```

Once the above code is set and executed, it should produce the following output:

```
20 times 100 is equal to 2000.0
```

String Concatenation

You can apply the + operator to concatenate two strings or a string and a character, or two characters. Here is a simple case:

```
let constA = "Hello,"
let constB = "World!"

var stringA = constA + constB
print (stringA)
```

Once the above code is executed, it should produce the following result:

```
Hello,World!
```

Typically, Swift strings do not have a length property, but you can use the global count() function to count the number of characters in a string in the following manner:

```
var varA = "Hello, Swift 4!"
print ("\(varA), length is\((varA.count))")
```

When the above code is set, it should output the following data:

```
Hello, Swift 4!, length is 15
```

String Comparison

In addition, you can insert the == operator to compare two strings variables or constants. To demonstrate:

```
var varA = "Hello, Swift 4!"
var varB = "Hello, World!"

if varA == varB {
   print ("\(varA) and\(varB) are equal")
} else {
   print ("\(varA) and\(varB) are not
equal")
}
```

When the above code is executed, it should result in the following variable:

Hello, Swift 4! and Hello, World! are not equal

String Iterating

Since strings are simply a collection of values it is possible to iterate over the string using loops in the following way:

```
for chars in "ThisString" {
print(chars, terminator: " ")
}
```

When the above code is compiled, it produces the following variable:

T h i s S t r i n g

String Functions and Operators

Swift is known to support a wide range of the following methods and operators related to strings:[6]

1. **isEmpty:** A Boolean value that specifies whether a string is empty or not.

2. **hasPrefix(prefix: String):** Function to see whether a given parameter string exists as a prefix of the string or not.

3. **hasSuffix(suffix: String):** Function to see whether a given parameter string exists as a suffix of the string or not.

4. **toInt():** Function to convert numeric String value into Integer.

5. **count():** Global function to count the number of characters in a string.

---

[6] https://www.tutorialspoint.com/swift/swift_strings.htm, Tutorialspoint

6. **utf8:** Property to return a UTF-8 representation of a string.

7. **utf16:** Property to return a UTF-16 representation of a string.

8. **unicodeScalars:** Property to return a Unicode Scalar representation of a string.

9. **+:** Operator to concatenate two strings, or a string and a character, or two characters.

10. **+=:** Operator to append a string or character to an existing string.

11. **==:** Operator to set the equality of two strings.

12. **<:** Operator to perform a lexicographical comparison to determine whether one string evaluates as less than another.

13. **startIndex:** Used to get the value at starting index of string.

14. **endIndex:** Used to get the value at ending index of string.

15. **Indices:** Applied to access all the characters of string one by one.

16. **insert("Value", at: position):** Applied to insert a value at a position.

17. **remove(at: position):** Used to remove a value at a position, or to remove a range of values from string.

18. **reversed():** Returns the reverse of a string.

As already mentioned, a character in Swift is a single character string literal, addressed by the data type Character. Take a look at the following example using two Character constants:

```
let char1: Character = "A"
let char2: Character = "B"

print("Value of char1 \(char1)")
print("Value of char2 \(char2)")
```

Once the above code is implemented, it produces the following result:

Value of char1 A

Value of char2 B

If you try to store more than one character in a Character type variable or constant, then Swift 4 will not allow that. Try to type the following example in Swift 4 Playground and you will get an error even before compilation.

```
// Following is wrong in Swift 4
let char: Character = "AB"
print("Value of char \(char)")
```

Empty Character Variables

Keep in mind that it is simply not possible to create an empty Character variable or constant which will have an empty value. Therefore, the following syntax is not valid:

```
// Following is wrong in Swift 4
let char1: Character = ""
var char2: Character = ""
```

```
print("Value of char1 \(char1)")
print("Value of char2 \(char2)")
```

Accessing Characters from Strings

As discussed earlier, String represents a collection of Character values in a specified order. So you can access individual characters from any given String by iterating over that string with a for-in loop in the following manner:

```
for ch in "Hello" {
    print(ch)
}
```

When the above code is executed, the end result will look like this:

```
H

e

l

l

o
```

Concatenating Strings with Characters

By looking at the following example you can see how a Swift Character can be concatenated with Swift String:

```
var varA:String = "Hello "
let varB:Character = "G"
varA.append (varB)

print("Value of varC = \(varA)")
```

Once the above code is fully executed, it shall produce this variable:

```
Value of var = Hello G
```

BUILDING AND RUNNING PROGRAMS ON C++

C++ is a low-level programming language that has been used for over 35 years now. And whilst C++ is a relatively old and complicated language, it is still very much relevant nowadays. C++ is predominantly utilized when higher performance is required. Examples of such complex conduct are the libraries used for Unreal Engine gaming or the execution of OpenCV live computer vision. As a matter of fact, Apple still employs C++ to script some of its most popular and performance-requiring features like MacRumour that is the Animoji feature written entirely in C++.

If you are building some C++ features in your Swift iOS app then looking to consume C++ from Swift, then you will find this section rather helpful. At this point, we shall assume that you know the basics of iOS development and Swift programming. There is no need to know C++ programming in detail, just the basics of Object-Oriented Programming. The C++ code that we are going to apply here is very basic and easy to grasp.

In this part of this chapter, we will first cover how to create a SwiftUI app from scratch. We will then add some C++ that returns "Hello from CPP world!" message. And finally, retrieve the "Hello from CPP world!" message and display it to the user.

Compiling a C++ program involves taking the source code you have at disposal (.cpp, .c, .h, .hpp files) and converting them into an executable or library that can run on a specified platform. This process can be divided into three main stages:

- Preprocessing
- Compilation
- Linking

Preprocessing

C++ has preprocessor directives that are marked in code with the prefix #, that set behaviors that are to be executed on the source code before its compiled. The first stage of compiling a C++ program, using the preprocessor, involves carrying out these behaviors.

The exact complexion of what the preprocessor does depends on the preprocessor directive. For instance, we tend to split code into separate files to make it easier to organize and read. In order to link code in one file with that in another, you should insert the #include directive. When compiling the C++ program, the preprocessor takes this #include and copies and pastes the code defined in that header file into the file that is including it. This saves time and prevents any potential errors from occurring as well as removes the necessity to copy code manually between files.

By the end of the preprocessor stage, all preprocessor directives in your code should be organized by the compiler preprocessor, and the outputted code would now be ready for the compiling stage.

Compiling

Compiling is the next step in the process and is related to turning the source code that we write into something that a computer can comprehend, which is machine code.

C++ compilation is itself a two-step process. First, the compiler takes the source code and converts it into assembly language. Assembly language could be defined as a low-level programming language that closely resembles the machine instructions of a central processing unit (CPU). Second, the source code now converted into assembly language is converted again into actual machine code via the assembler. Machine code consists of instructions scripted in binary, described as machine language because the CPU can actually understand it. The resulting product is a set of files stored in an intermediary file format, also known as an object file.

An object file typically has the .obj or .o file extension and is created for each source code file. The object file contains all of the machine-level instructions for that file. It is referred to as an intermediary file because it is not until the final stage, linking, that an actual executable or library that we can use is created.

It is at the compilation stage that we will be warned about any errors in our code that might cause compilation failure. Any errors that occur are typically happening due to the compiler not registering the code that we have written. Common error examples are missing a semi-colon, miss-spelling a C++ keyword, or adding one too many curly braces to the end of a method. If an error is found, then compilation is stopped entirely. Meaning that you will not be able to compile your C++ code until all errors are fixed. Without it, your code will not be recognizable C++ basically messing up the overall syntax.

Linking

The final stage of the process is linking, which is basically taking our output from the previous step and linking it all together to produce the actual executable or library.

The first step in this stage is compiling all of the object files into an executable or library. A library here stands for a reusable collection of functions, classes, and objects that share a common purpose, for example, a math library. Once this has been successfully completed, the next step is linking this executable with any external libraries that you want to include in your program.

Finally, the linker has to resolve any dependencies. This is where any errors relating to linking typically take place. Common errors include not being able to find a library specified, or trying to link two files that might, for example, both have a class that shares the same name. Assuming no errors occur during this stage, you will have an executable file or library ready by the compiler.

Fundamentally Swift cannot consume C++ code directly. However, Swift is capable of consuming Objective-C code, and Objective-C (more specifically its variant Objective-C++) code is able to consume C++. Therefore, in order for Swift code to consume C++ code, you should create an Objective-C wrapper or bridging code.

1. **Creating an iOS SwiftUI app from scratch:** Let us start by creating a new SwiftUI app for iOS. Open Xcode and create a new project using the iOS

template. On "Choose options for your new project" prompt call the app SwiftCPP. Make sure the
"Interface:" option is SwiftUI, "Life Cycle:" is SwiftUI
App, and finally the "Language:" is set to Swift. All
other checkboxes can be left unchecked.

At last, navigate to a folder where you would like to
store your project and click Create.

2. **Adding C++ code:** Next, you should add some C++
code. From the menu, select File, and once prompted
to "Choose a template for your new file" search and
select C++ File under the iOS tab.

Next name the file HelloWorld and check "Also
create a header file." When prompted "Would you
like to configure an Objective-C bridging header?"
make sure to select Create Bridging Header.

The bridging header is where you need to
specify Xcode which Objective-C code you want
to be consumed from Swift later. From here just
add some C++ code to our HelloWorld files. First,
open the header file that is like the protocol or
interface and then dd the following code under
#include <stdio.h>:

```
#include <string>
class HelloWorld {
public:
    std::string sayHello();
};
```

After that, you are expected to add the implementation of the HelloWorld interface. Open HelloWorld.

cpp and under #include "HelloWorld.hpp" insert the following code:

```
std::string HelloWorld::sayHello() {
    return "Hello from CPP world!";
}
```

3. **Creating C++ Bridging code:** As mentioned earlier, it is not possible to consume C++ code from Swift directly. Rather Swift can consume Objective-C and Objective-C can consume C++. Thus, we need to create a wrapper or bridging code between Swift and C++ in Objective-C.

   Let us start by adding a new file from the File menu. Next search and select Header File from the iOS tab. Here just name the file HelloWorldWrapper then click Create. Replace the file content to the following:

```
#import <Foundation/Foundation.h>
@interface HelloWorldWrapper: NSObject
- (NSString *) sayHello;
@end
```

After that, you need to create the implementation file of the HelloWorldWrapper interface. From the File menu, search and select Objective-C File from the iOS tab. Next name the file HelloWorldWrapper and click Create.

   Once that is done, change the file name from HelloWorldWrapper.m to HelloWorldWrapper.mm. The second "m" in HelloWorldWrapper.mm signals Xcode and the compiler that this Objective-C file will use C++ code.

Then add an "m" to the extension of the file name and add the following code under #import <Foundation/Foundation.h> statement:

```
#import "HelloWorldWrapper.h"
#import "HelloWorld.hpp"
@implementation HelloWorldWrapper
- (NSString *) sayHello {
    HelloWorld helloWorld;
    std::string helloWorldMessage =
helloWorld.sayHello();
    return [NSString
            stringWithCString:helloWor
ldMessage.c_str()
            encoding:NSUTF8StringEncod
ing];
}
@end
```

With the above code, we are simply calling the C++ code and converting a C++ string to an Objective-C NSString.

4. **Consuming C++ code from Swift:** Now that you have the C++ code wrapped in Objective-C, the Objective-C wrapper is not yet ready to be consumed. First, you need to signal Xcode that you wish to consume the Objective-C code in Swift. To do this, you must auto-create SwiftCPP-Bridging-Header.h and add the following line:

```
#import "HelloWorldWrapper.h"
```

This tells Xcode to automatically create a Swift binding interface for the HelloWorldWrapper Objective-C code. With that, you are all set to consume the Objective-C code. Open ContentView.swift and convert the following code:

```
struct ContentView: View {
    var body: some View {
        Text("Hello, world!").padding()
    }
}
to:
struct ContentView: View {
    var body: some View {
        Text(HelloWorldWrapper().
sayHello()).padding()
    }
}
```

The main difference here is that instead of displaying "Hello, world!" we are now retrieving the message from the Objective-C HelloWorld wrapper by calling HelloWorldWrapper().sayHello().

Now you can run the app on a simulator and see it operating while consuming C++ code from Swift.

USING THE REPL

A read–eval–print loop (REPL), which is also called a language shell could be best defined as a simple, interactive computer programming environment that takes single user inputs, evaluates them, and prints the result to the user. Swift REPL is built on LLDB and Xcode playgrounds are built on it.

Developers familiar with interpreted languages will feel comfortable in this command-line environment, and even experienced developers will find a few unique features. To get started, launch Terminal.app and type "swift" at the prompt in OS X Yosemite, or "xcrun swift" in OS X Mavericks. You will then be in the Swift REPL:

Welcome to Swift version 1.1 (swift-600.0.20.0). Type: help for assistance.

1>

All you need to do is type Swift statements and the REPL will immediately execute your code. Expression results will be automatically set and displayed along with their type, as are the results of both variable and constant declarations. Console result will naturally feature within the interactive session in the following manner:

```
  1> "100".toInt()
$R0: Int? = 100
  2> let name = "Jane"
name: String = "Jane"
  3> println("Hello, \(name)")
Hello, Jane
```

Keep in mind that the result from line one has been given a name by the REPL even though the result of the expression was not explicitly assigned to anything. You can address these results to reuse their values in following statements:

```
  4> $R0! + 100
$R1: Int = 200
```

The Swift compiler recognizes incomplete code and will prompt for extra input when needed. Your code might even get omitted automatically as it would in Xcode. To illustrate, starting a function:

```
5> func timesTwo() {
6.
```

The prompt for continuation lines is a line number followed by a period instead of the angle bracket that identified a new statement, so you can tell for sure when you are being asked to complete a code fragment. At this point you can keep scripting the remaining lines in the method:

```
5> func timesTwo() {
6.              return value * 2
7. }
```

There are three noteworthy remarks to make here: the first is that line six was originally ignored, but the REPL automatically included it when you typed the closing brace. The second is that the function references a parameter we did not declare and that needs a return type, so you should add both to the declaration. The last is that even if you did insert return after the last line, it is never too late to edit it shall you change your mind.

Multiline History

Once code is submitted to the compiler it is also automatically recorded in the REPL history, which makes correcting mistakes problematic. If you pressed return at the end of the incomplete function declaration above, you would get the follow-up with the message stating:

error: use of unresolved identifier "value"

Like most history implementations, you can call up your last entry by pressing up the arrow from the prompt. The REPL then shall bring back our last example, and place the cursor at the end implying that you can now proceed with editing the code to correct your mistake.

Your history is preserved between sessions and will record hundreds of code components. Each time you move up from the top line, you will go on to an earlier history entry. And each time you move down from an empty line at the bottom of an entry, you will go back to a more recent history entry.

Multiline Editing

Although the REPL behaves like a traditional line editor most of the time, it also provides unique features for managing multi-line input like most class or function declarations. In the example above, before pressing return on the final line you could also press up arrow to shift the cursor up to the declaration line, then use the left arrow to move the cursor just after the opening parenthesis for the parameter list:

```
5> func timesTwo() {
6.          return value * 2
7. }
```

Here you can type the parameter declaration, press the right arrow to move past the closing parenthesis, and insert the return type as well:

```
5> func timesTwo(value: Int) -> Int {
6.            return value * 2
7. }
```

Nevertheless, you cannot press return to complete the declaration at this point because you are in the middle of a block of text. Pressing return would simply insert a line break, which can be helpful only when you are trying to insert additional lines in a function or method body, but what you want here is to move to the end of the declaration. You can press the down arrow twice to get there or use the ESC escape key followed by a closing angle bracket. Pressing return at the end of the last line will compile the newly declared function so it is prompted for further use:

```
 8> timesTwo(20)
$R2: (Int) = 40
```

Automatic detection of statement completion means that you can just type code and the REPL will do the right thing most of the time. There are instances, however, where it is necessary to submit more than one declaration at the same time because they have mutual dependencies. Review the following code:

```
func foo() {
     bar()
}
func bar() {
     foo()
}
```

Scripting everything above line by line will result in trying to compile the first function once the third line is complete, and of course, this produces an error:

error: use of unresolved identifier "bar"

Instead, you could declare both functions on a single line to activate around automatic completion detection that takes place when you press return. At the same time, there is a better solution. After typing the third line above, you can press the down arrow to move to create a fourth line manually, and type the remainder normally. The two declarations would be compiled together, achieving the desired goal of mutual recursion.

Quick Reference

To help you get started, there are most commonly used editing and navigation keys you can apply:[7]

1. Arrow Keys	Move cursor left/right/up/down	
2. Control+F	Move cursor right one character, same as right arrow	
3. Control+B	Move cursor left one character, same as left arrow	
4. Control+N	Move cursor to end of next line, same as down arrow	

---

[7] https://developer.apple.com/swift/blog/?id=18, Apple

5. Control+P   Move cursor to end of prior line, same as up arrow

6. Control+D   Delete the character under the cursor

7. Option+Left   Move cursor to start of prior word

8. Option+Right   Move cursor to start of next word

9. Control+A   Move cursor to start of current line

10. Control+E   Move cursor to end of current line

11. Delete   Delete the character to the left of the cursor

12. Esc <   Move cursor to start of first line

13. Esc >   Move cursor to end of last line

To summarize, in this chapter, we have discussed the Basic Swift Language Syntax and learned how to interact with the REPL tool. In addition, we have established how you can manage various data types such as Strings, Ints, Floats, and Bools. In the next chapter, we shall focus on Swift variables and constants, as well as Objects, Classes, and Enumerations.

Swift Basic Syntax

IN THIS CHAPTER

> ➤ Learning about Swift variables and constants

> ➤ Setting objects and classes

> ➤ Using and modifying enumerations and functions

In the preceding chapters, you learned Swift's technical requirements, installation process, and main data types; in this chapter, you will review Swift's basic syntax in detail, learn about its components and widgets.

Let us start by recollecting some of the previous material. Fundamentally, we have established that many parts of Swift might be familiar from your experience of developing in C and Objective-C. Thus, Swift provides its own versions of all fundamental C and Objective-C types, including Int for integers, Double and Float for floating-point values, Bool for Boolean values, and String for textual data.

DOI: 10.1201/9781003254089-3

Like C, Swift uses variables to store and refer to values by an identifying name. Swift also makes extensive use of variables whose values cannot be changed. These are known as constants, and are much more flexible than constants in C. Constants are used throughout Swift to make code safer and cleaner in intent when you work with values that do not need to change.

In addition to familiar types discussed in Chapter 2, Swift introduces advanced types not found in Objective-C, such as tuples. Tuples enable you to create and forward groupings of different values. You can also use a tuple to return multiple values from a function as a single compound value.

We have also introduced optional types, which handle the absence of a value. Optionals usually state that either "there is a value, and it equals x" or "there is no value at all." Using optionals is similar to using nil with pointers in Objective-C, but they work for any type, not just classes. Not only are optionals safer and more expressive than nil pointers in Objective-C, but they are also at the core of many of Swift's most powerful features.

Since Swift is a type-safe language, it naturally helps you to be clear about the types of values your code can work with. For instance, if part of your code requires a String, type safety prevents you from passing it an Int by mistake. Likewise, type safety prevents you from accidentally passing an optional String to a code that requires a non-optional String. Type safety can also help you catch and fix errors as early as possible in the development process.

VARIABLES AND CONSTANTS

Constants and variables are used to identify a name (such as maximumNumberOfLoginAttempts or welcomeMessage) with a value of a particular type (such as the number 10 or the string "Hello"). At the same time, the value of a constant cannot be changed once it is set, whereas a variable can be set to a different value in the long run.

Declaring Constants and Variables

As a standard, constants and variables should be declared before they are used. You must declare constants with the let keyword and variables with the var keyword. To illustrate with an example of how constants and variables can be applied to track the number of login attempts a user has made:

```
let maximumNumberOfLoginAttempts = 5
var currentLoginAttempt = 0
```

This message can be decoded as:

"Declare a new constant called maximumNumberOfLoginAttempts, and assign it a value of 5. Next, declare a new variable called currentLoginAttempt, and give it an initial value of 0."

In this case, the maximum number of allowed login attempts is declared as a constant, because the maximum value never changes. The current login attempt counter is set as a variable because this value must be incremented after each failed login attempt.

In addition, you can also declare multiple constants or multiple variables on a single line, separated by commas:

```
var x = 0.0, y = 0.0, z = 0.0
```

In case a stored value in your code will not change, make sure to declare it as a constant with the let keyword. And use variables only for storing values that need to be modified in the future.

Type Annotations

It is possible to include a type annotation when you declare a constant or variable, to be clear about the kind of values the constant or variable can store. You can write a type annotation by placing a colon after the constant or variable name, followed by a space, followed by the name of the type to use. Here is an example that provides a type annotation for a variable called welcomeMessage, to state that the variable can store String values:

```
var welcomeMessage: String
```

You can also determine multiple related variables of the same type on a single line, separated by commas, with a single type annotation after the final variable name:

```
var red, green, blue: Double
```

Nevertheless, it is rare that you would be required to write type annotations in practice. If you provide an initial value for a constant or variable at the point that it is defined,

Swift can almost always independently infer the type to be used for that constant or variable.

Naming Constants and Variables

By default, constant and variable names can hold almost any character, including Unicode characters:

```
let π = 3.14159
let 🐶🐮 = "dogcow"
```

However, keep in mind that the same constant and variable names cannot contain whitespace characters, mathematical symbols, arrows, private-use Unicode scalar values, or line- and box-drawing components. Nor can they begin with a number, although numbers may be inserted elsewhere within the name. Once you have set a constant or variable of a certain type, you cannot reset it again with the same name, or modify it to store values of a different type. Nor can you edit a constant into a variable or a variable into a constant.

In case you need to give a constant or variable the same name as a reserved Swift keyword, simply surround the keyword with backticks (`) when using it as a name. You can change the value of an existing variable to another value of a compatible type. Yet make sure to avoid using keywords as names unless you have no other option. In this example, the value of friendlyWelcome is changed from "Hello!" to "Ciao!":

```
var friendlyWelcome = "Hello!"
friendlyWelcome = "Ciao!"
// friendlyWelcome is now "Ciao!"
```

Unlike a variable, the value of a constant cannot be edited once you set it. Attempting to do so will result in the following error:

```
let languageName = "Swift"
languageName = "Swift++"
// This is a compile-time error:
languageName cannot be changed.
```

Printing Constants and Variables

It is possible to print the current value of a constant or variable with the print(_:separator:terminator:) function:

```
print(friendlyWelcome)
// Prints "Ciao!"
```

This print(_:separator:terminator:) function is also referred to as a global function that prints one or more values to an appropriate output. In Xcode, for instance, the print(_:separator:terminator:) function prints its output in Xcode's "console" platform. The separator and terminator parameters have default values, so you can ignore them when you call this function. By default, the function closes the line it prints by including a line break. To print a value without a line break after it, just pass an empty string as the terminator—to demonstrate: print(someValue, terminator: "").

Swift also utilizes string interpolation to add the name of a constant or variable as a placeholder in a longer string and to prompt Swift to replace it with the current value of that constant or variable. Simply wrap the name in parentheses and end it with a backslash before the opening parenthesis:

```
print("The current value of friendlyWelcome
is \(friendlyWelcome)")
// Prints "The current value of
friendlyWelcome is Ciao!"
```

CONDITIONS AND LOOPS

Swift has a variety of control flow statements. These include while loops that complete a task automatically multiple times; if, guard, and switch statements to activate different parts of code based on certain conditions; and statements such as break and continue to transfer the flow of implementation to another item in your code. Swift also provides a for-in loop that makes it easy to iterate over arrays, dictionaries, ranges, strings, and other components.

Swift's switch statement is considerably more versatile than its counterpart in many C-like languages. Cases can match many different patterns, including interval matches, tuples, and casts to a particular type. Matched values in a switch case can be bound to temporary constants or variables for use within the case's body, and complex matching conditions can be indicated through a where clause for each case.

For-In Loops

You apply the for-in loop to iterate over a sequence, such as items in an array, ranges of numbers, or characters in a string.

This example adds a for-in loop to iterate over the items in an array:

```
let names = ["Maria", "Alex," "Bob," "John"]
for name in names {
    print("Hello, \(name)!")
}
// Hello, Maria!
// Hello, Alex!
// Hello, Bob!
// Hello, John!
```

You can also iterate over a dictionary to be able to use its key-value pairs. Each item in the dictionary is returned as a (key, value) tuple when the dictionary is iterated, and you can decompose the (key, value) tuple's components as explicitly named constants for use within the body of the for-in loop. In the code below, the dictionary's keys are decomposed into a constant called animalName, and the dictionary's values are decomposed into a constant called legCount:[1]

```
let numberOfLegs = ["spider": 8, "ant": 6,
"cat": 4]
for (animalName, legCount) in numberOfLegs {
    print("\(animalName)s have\(legCount)
legs")
}
//cats have 4 legs
//ants have 6 legs
//spiders have 8 legs
```

---

[1] https://docs.swift.org/swift-book/LanguageGuide/ControlFlow.html, Swift

The contents of a Dictionary are naturally out of order, and iterating over them will not guarantee the same retrieval order. To put it simply, the order you insert items into a Dictionary does not determine the order they are iterated.

Nevertheless, you can also use for-in loops with numeric ranges. This example displays the first few entries in a five-time table:[2]

```swift
for index in 1...5 {
    print("\(index) times 5 is \(index * 5)")
}
// 1 times 5 is 5
// 2 times 5 is 10
// 3 times 5 is 15
// 4 times 5 is 20
// 5 times 5 is 25
```

The sequence being iterated over is a range of numbers from one to five, inclusive, as marked by the use of the closed range operator (...). In the example above, the index comes as a constant whose value is automatically set at the start of each iteration of the loop. As such, the index does not have to be declared before it is applied. It is implicitly declared simply by its inclusion in the loop declaration, without the need for a let declaration keyword.

---

[2] https://docs.swift.org/swift-book/LanguageGuide/ControlFlow.html, Swift

While Loops

A while loop compasses a set of statements until a condition becomes false. This type of loops is best used when the number of iterations is not known before the first iteration commences. Swift provides two kinds of while loops:

- **while:** Evaluates its condition at the beginning of each pass through the loop.

- **for-in:** This loop carries a set of statements for each item in a range, sequence, collection, or progression.

- **repeat while loop:** Similar to the while statement, except that it tests the condition at the end of the loop body.

A while loop starts by estimating a single condition. In case the condition is true, a set of statements is repeated until the condition becomes false. The general form of a while loop has the following shape:

```
while condition {
    statements
}
```

The other variation of the while loop, the repeat-while loop, completes a single pass through the loop block first, before considering the loop's condition, and continues to do so until the condition is false. Here is the general form of a repeat-while loop:

```
repeat {
    statements
} while condition
```

Loop Control Statements

Loop control statements change implementation from its normal sequence. When execution leaves a scope, all automatic objects that were produced in that scope are removed. Swift naturally supports the following control statements:

- **continue statement:** This statement dictates a loop to stop what it is doing and start again at the beginning of the next iteration through the loop.

- **break statement:** Terminates the loop statement and transfers implementation to the statement following the loop.

- **fallthrough statement:** The fallthrough statement imitates the behavior of Swift switch to C-style switch.

Conditional Statements

Conditional statements are most useful when executing different pieces of code based on certain conditions. You might want to run an extra piece of code when an error occurs, or to display a message when a value becomes too high or too low. To do this, you should make parts of your code conditional.

Swift has two ways to add conditional branches to your code: The if statement and the switch statement. Normally, you apply the if statement to estimate simple conditions with only a few potential outcomes. The switch statement is suitable to more complicated conditions with multiple possible options and is useful in cases where pattern matching can assist in selecting an appropriate code branch to operate.

If

In its simplest shape, the if statement can have a single if condition. It goes through a set of statements only if that condition is true. To illustrate with an example:

```
var temperatureInFahrenheit = 20
if temperatureInFahrenheit <= 30 {
    print("It's very cold. Consider wearing
a sweater.")
}
// Prints "It's very cold. Consider wearing
a sweater."
```

The example above checks whether the temperature is less than or equal to 30 degrees Fahrenheit and in case it is, a message is displayed. Otherwise, there will be no message, and code execution shall go on continues after the if statement's closing brace.

In addition, the if statement can provide an alternative set of statements, known as an else clause, for situations when the if condition is false. These statements are identified by the else keyword:

```
temperatureInFahrenheit = 40
if temperatureInFahrenheit <= 30 {
    print("It's very cold. Consider wearing
a sweater.")
} else {
    print("It's not that cold. Wear a
t-shirt.")
}
// Prints "It's not that cold. Wear a
t-shirt."
```

One of these two branches should be executed. Since the temperature has increased to 40 degrees Fahrenheit, it is no longer cold enough to recommend wearing a sweater, and so the else branch is activated instead. You can link multiple if statements together to consider additional clauses in the following manner:[3]

```
temperatureInFahrenheit = 90
if temperatureInFahrenheit <= 30 {
    print("It's very cold. Consider wearing
a sweater.")
} else if temperatureInFahrenheit >= 86 {
    print("It's really warm. Do not forget
to wear sunscreen.")
} else {
    print("It's not that cold. Wear a
t-shirt.")
}
// Prints "It's really warm. Do not forget
to wear sunscreen."
```

As you can observe, an additional if statement was added to respond to particularly warm temperatures. The final else clause remains, and it displays a response for any temperatures that are neither too warm nor too cold. It is an optional clause; however, it can be excluded if the set of conditions does not need to be complete.

---

[3] https://docs.swift.org/swift-book/LanguageGuide/ControlFlow.html, Swift

Switch

A switch statement identifies a value and compares it against several possible matching patterns. It then implements an appropriate block of code, based on the first pattern that matches successfully. A switch statement has an alternative to the if statement for responding to multiple potential states. To put it simply, a switch statement compares a value against one or more values of the same type as demonstrated here:

```
switch some value to consider {
case value 1:
    respond to value 1
case value 2,
    value 3:
    respond to value 2 or 3
default:
    otherwise, do something else
}
```

Every switch statement can have multiple possible cases, each of which starts with the case keyword. In addition to comparing against specific values, Swift offers several ways for each case to select more complex matching patterns. Like the body of an if statement, each case is an independent branch of code execution and the switch statement decides which branch should be selected. This procedure is also referred to as switching on the value that is being considered.

Every switch statement is exhaustive in its nature. Meaning that every possible value of the type being considered should be paired by one of the switch cases. In case it is not appropriate to provide a case for every possible value, you can define a default case to match any values that are not reviewed explicitly. This default case is marked by the default keyword, and should always come last.

Unlike switch statements in C and Objective-C, switch statements in Swift do not automatically fall through the bottom of each case and into the next one. Instead, the entire switch statement completes its execution as soon as the first matching switch case is over, without requiring an additional break statement. This makes the switch statement easier to apply than the one in C and prevents implementing more than one switch case by mistake.

Even if break is not required in Swift, you can still insert a break statement to match and omit a particular case or to break out of a matched case before that case has finished its execution. The body of each case should hold at least one executable statement. It is not acceptable to script the following code, because the first case is empty:

```
let anotherCharacter: Character = "a"
switch anotherCharacter {
case "a": // Invalid, the case has an empty
body
case "A":
    print("The letter A")
default:
    print("Not the letter A")
}
// This will report a compile-time error.
```

In contrast with a switch statement in C, this switch statement does not match both "a" and "A." Instead, it reports a compile-time error that case "a": does not have any executable statements. This approach avoids accidental fallthrough from one case to another and makes for secure code that is cleaner in its intent.

In case you need to make a switch with a single case that matches both "a" and "A," simply combine the two values into a compound case, separating the values with commas:

```
let anotherCharacter: Character = "a"
switch anotherCharacter {
case "a", "A":
    print("The letter A")
default:
    print("Not the letter A")
}
// Prints "The letter A"
```

Please note that for better readability, a compound case can also be scripted over multiple lines.

Control Transfer Statements

Control transfer statements are used to change the order in which your code is implemented, by transferring control from one piece of code to another. Swift has five control transfer statements:

- continue

- break

- fallthrough

- return

- throw

We shall look into continue, break, and fallthrough statements in this section. The return statement and the throw statement are described under Functions part of this chapter.

Continue

The continue statement basically tells a loop to stop what it is doing and start again at the beginning of the next iteration through the loop. It forwards the message saying "I am finished with the current loop iteration" without dropping the loop altogether. The following example removes all vowels and spaces from a lowercase string to create a cryptic puzzle phrase:[4]

```
let puzzleInput = "great minds think alike"
var puzzleOutput = ""
let charactersToRemove: [Character] = ["a",
"e", "i", "o", "u", " "]
for character in puzzleInput {
    if charactersToRemove.
contains(character) {
        continue
    }
    puzzleOutput.append(character)
}
print(puzzleOutput)
// Prints "grtmndsthnklk"
```

You could see how the code above uses the continue keyword whenever it matches a vowel or a space, causing the current iteration of the loop to end immediately and to start the next iteration.

---

[4] https://docs.swift.org/swift-book/LanguageGuide/ControlFlow.html, Swift

Break

The break statement is applied to end the execution of an entire control flow statement immediately. It can be used inside a switch or loop statement when you need to terminate the execution of the switch or loop statement earlier than would otherwise be the case.

Break in a Loop Statement When applied inside a loop statement, break ends the loop's execution at once and transfers control to the code after the loop's closing brace (}). No further code from the current iteration of the loop is reviewed, and no further iterations of the loop are initiated.

Break in a Switch Statement When applied inside a switch statement, break causes the switch statement to end its execution straight away and to transfer control to the code after the switch statement's closing brace (}).

This pattern can be used to match and omit one or more cases in a switch statement. Because Swift's switch statement is exhaustive and does not accept empty cases, it is at times necessary to intentionally match and ignore a case in order to make your intentions explicit. You can do this by writing the break statement as the entire body of the case you need to omit. When that case is matched by the switch statement, the break statement inside the case instantly ends the switch statement's execution.

Fallthrough

As previously mentioned, switch statements do not typically fall through the bottom of each case and into the next one. That is, the entire switch statement completes its execution as soon as the first matching case is over with. By contrast, C requires you to include an explicit break statement at the end of every switch case to prevent fallthrough. Avoiding default fallthrough means that Swift switch statements are much more concise and predictable than their counterparts in C, and thus they avoid running multiple switch cases by mistake.

In case you need C-style fallthrough behavior, you can opt into this behavior on a case-by-case basis with the fallthrough keyword. The example below uses fallthrough to create a textual description of the following number:[5]

```
let integerToDescribe = 5
var description = "The number
\(integerToDescribe) is"
switch integerToDescribe {
case 2, 3, 5, 7, 11, 13, 17, 19:
    description += " a prime number, and
also"
    fallthrough
default:
    description += " an integer."
}
print(description)
// Prints "The number 5 is a prime number,
and also an integer."
```

---

[5] https://docs.swift.org/swift-book/LanguageGuide/ControlFlow.html, Swift

This example results in a new String variable called description and assigns it an initial value. The function then reviews the value of integerToDescribe using a switch statement. If the value of integerToDescribe is one of the prime numbers in the list, the function sends text to the end of the description, to note that the number is prime. It then uses the fallthrough keyword to "fall into" the default case as well. The default case adds an extra note to the end of the description, and with that the switch statement is complete.

Unless the value of integerToDescribe is in the list of known prime numbers, it is not matched by the first switch case at all. And since there are no other specific cases, integerToDescribe is matched by the default case. Once the switch statement has finished administering, the number's description is printed using the print(_:separator:terminator:) function. In this above example, the number 5 is therefore correctly identified as a prime number.

At the same time, the fallthrough keyword does not check the case conditions for the switch case that it causes execution to fall into. The fallthrough keyword simply causes code execution to move directly to the statements inside the next case (or default case) block, similar to the C's standard switch statement behavior.

Labeled Statements

In Swift, it is possible to place loops and conditional statements inside other loops and conditional statements to produce complex control flow structures. However, loops and conditional statements can both apply the break statement to end their execution prematurely. Therefore, it could be useful to be clear about which exact loop or conditional statement you need a break statement to terminate. Additionally, if you have multiple nested loops, it can be helpful to be straightforward about which loop the continue statement should impact on.

In order to achieve these tasks, you can attribute a loop statement or conditional statement with a statement label. With a conditional statement, you can insert a statement label with the break statement to end the execution of the labeled statement. For a loop statement, you can include a statement label with the break or continue statement to end or continue the execution of the labeled statement.

A labeled statement is registered by placing a label on the same line as the statement's opening keyword, followed by a colon. Here's a simple illustration of this syntax for a while loop, although the pattern is the same for all loops and switch statements:

```
label name: while condition {
    statements
}
```

Early Exit

A guard statement, similar to an if statement, runs statements depending on the Boolean value of an expression. You use a guard statement to require that a condition must be true in order for the code after the guard statement to be implemented. Yet unlike an if statement, a guard statement normally has an else clause—the code inside the else clause is executed if the condition is not true:

```
func greet(person: [String: String]) {
    guard let name = person["name"] else {
        return
    }
    print("Hello\(name)!")

    guard let location = person["location"] else {
        print("I hope the weather is nice near you.")
        return
    }
    print("I hope the weather is nice in \(location).")
}
greet(person: ["name": "Jack"])
// Prints "Hello Jack!"
// Prints "I hope the weather is nice near you."
greet(person: ["name": "Mary", "location": "New York"])
// Prints "Hello Mary!"
// Prints "I hope the weather is nice in New York."
```

If the guard statement's condition is acceptable, code execution runs after the guard statement's closing brace. Any variables or constants that were connected values using an optional binding as part of the condition are available for the rest of the code block that the guard statement appears in.

However, if that condition is not acceptable, the code inside the else branch is executed. That branch would then be expected to transfer control to exit the code block in which the guard statement locates. It can do this via control transfer statements such as return, break, continue, or throw, or it can call a function or method that does not return, such as fatalError(_:file:line:).

As a side note, using a guard statement is said to improve the overall readability of your code, compared to doing the same check with an if statement. It lets you script the code that is typically implemented without wrapping it in an else block, and it allows you to keep the code that administers a violated requirement next to the general requirement.

Checking API Availability

Swift is known for its built-in support for checking Application Programming Interface (API) availability, which ensures that you do not accidentally use APIs that are unavailable on a given setup target.

The compiler uses availability information in the software development kit (SDK) to confirm that all of the APIs in your code are available on the setup target specified in your project. At the same time, Swift will report an error at compile time if you try and use an API that is not available.

You can use an availability condition in an if or guard statement to conditionally implement a block of code, depending on whether the APIs you need to use are available at runtime. The compiler uses the information from the availability condition when it confirms that the APIs in that block of code are available:

```
if #available(iOS 10, macOS 10.12, *) {
    // Use iOS 10 APIs on iOS, and use
macOS 10.12 APIs on macOS
} else {
    // Fall back to earlier iOS and macOS
APIs
}
```

The availability condition above states that in iOS, the body of the if statement runs only in iOS 10 and later; in macOS, only in macOS 10.12 and later. The last argument, *, is required and identifies that on any other platform, the body of the if administers on the minimum setup target stated by your target.

In its basic form, the availability condition uses a list of platform names and versions. You create platform names such as iOS, macOS, watchOS, and tvOS. In addition to specifying major version numbers like iOS 8 or macOS 10.10, you can also add minor versions numbers like iOS 11.2.6 and macOS 10.13.3.:

```
if #available(platform name version, …, *) {
    statements to execute if the APIs are
available
} else {
    fallback statements to execute if the
APIs are unavailable
}
```

FUNCTIONS

Functions are self-contained bits of code that perform a particular task. You give a function a name that goes with what it does, and this name will be used to "call" the function to complete its task when needed.

Swift's unified function syntax is versatile enough to complete anything from a simple C-style function with no parameter names to a complex Objective-C-style method with names and argument labels for each parameter. Parameters also offer default values to simplify function calls and can be treated as in-out parameters, which modify a passed variable once the function has finished its execution.

As a matter of fact, every function in Swift has a type, consisting of the function's parameter types and return type. You can utilize this type like any other type in Swift, which makes it easy to pass functions as parameters to other functions and to return functions from functions. Functions can also be inserted within other functions to be able to hold useful functionality within a nested function scope.

Defining and Calling Functions

When you define a function, you can also define one or more named, typed values that the function takes as input, known as parameters. It is also possible to define a type of value that the function will display as output when it is done, known as its return type.

Every function has an assigned function name, which defines the task that the function performs. In order to use a function, you "call" that function with its name and forward it input values (also known as arguments) that match the types of the function's parameters. A function's arguments should always be presented in the same order as the function's parameter list. Let us illustrate this information with an example.

The function below is called greet(person:), because that is precisely what it does—it takes a person's name as input and returns a greeting for that person. To complete this, you define one input parameter—a String value called person—and a return type of String, which will hold a greeting for that person:

```
func greet(person: String) -> String {
    let greeting = "Hello, " + person + "!"
    return greeting
}
```

All of this information is located into the function's definition, which is prefixed with the func keyword. You just need to indicate the function's return type with the return arrow -> (a hyphen followed by a right angle bracket), which is followed by the name of the type to return.

The definition is naturally used to describe what the function does, what it expects to receive, and what it returns when it is done. Additionally, the definition makes it easy for the function to be called unambiguously from anywhere in your code:

```
print(greet(person: "Mary"))
// Prints "Hello, Mary!"
print(greet(person: "Jack"))
// Prints "Hello, Jack!"
```

As shown above, you call the greet(person:) function by passing it a String value after the person argument label, such as greet(person: "Mary"). And because the function returns a String value, greet(person:) can be wrapped in a call to the print(_:separator:terminator:) function to print that string and observe its return value.

The print(_:separator:terminator:) function does not have a label for its first argument, and its other arguments are optional because they have a default value. The body of the greet(person:) function starts with a new String constant called greeting and setting it to a simple greeting message. This greeting is then passed back out of the function using the return keyword. In the line of code that says return greeting, the function finishes its execution and returns the current value of greeting.

It is possible to call the greet(person:) function multiple times with different input values. The example above shows what happens if it is called with an input value of "Mary," and an input value of "Jack." The function returns a tailored greeting in each case and in case you want to make the body of this function shorter, you can modify the message creation and the return statement into one line as follows:

```
func greetAgain(person: String) -> String {
    return "Hello again, " + person + "!"
}
print(greetAgain(person: "Mary"))
// Prints "Hello again, Mary!"
```

Function Parameters and Return Values

Function parameters and return values are extremely alterable in Swift. You can define anything from a simple utility function with a single unnamed parameter to a complex function with expressive parameter names and different parameter options.

Functions without Parameters

These are functions that simply are not required to define input parameters. Here is a function without input parameters, which always returns the same string message whenever it is running:

```
func sayHelloWorld() -> String {
    return "hello, world"
}
print(sayHelloWorld())
// Prints "hello, world"
```

The important thing to note is that the function definition still needs parentheses after the function's name, even though it technically does not take any parameters. The function name is also followed by an empty pair of parentheses when the function is called.

Functions with Multiple Parameters

These are functions that can have multiple input parameters, which are written within the function's parentheses, separated by commas. This function typically takes a person's name and whether they have already been greeted as input, and returns the standard greeting for that person:

```
func greet(person: String, alreadyGreeted:
Bool) -> String {
    if alreadyGreeted {
        return greetAgain(person: person)
    } else {
        return greet(person: person)
    }
}
```

```
print(greet(person: "Jack", alreadyGreeted:
true))
// Prints "Hello again, Jack!"
```

As you can see, you call the greet(person:alreadyGreeted:) function by passing it both a String argument value labeled person and a Bool argument value labeled alreadyGreeted in parentheses, separated by commas. Keep in mind that this function is different from the greet(person:) function shown in an earlier section. Even if both functions have names that begin with greet, the greet(person:alreadyGreeted:) function can contain two arguments but the greet(person:) function holds only one.

Functions without Return Values
These functions are not required to define a return type. For instance, the following version of the greet(person:) function, can print its own String value instead of returning it:

```
func greet(person: String) {
    print("Hello, \(person)!")
}
greet(person: "Peter")
// Prints "Hello, Peter!"
```

Since there is no need to return a value, the function's definition does not have the return arrow (->) or a return type.

Functions with Multiple Return Values
It is acceptable to use a tuple type as the return type for a function to return multiple values as part of one compound

return value. The example below describes a function named minMax(array:), which finds the smallest and largest numbers in an array of Int values:[6]

```swift
func minMax(array: [Int]) -> (min: Int,
max: Int) {
    var currentMin = array[0]
    var currentMax = array[0]
    for value in array[1..<array.count] {
        if value < currentMin {
            currentMin = value
        } else if value > currentMax {
            currentMax = value
        }
    }
    return (currentMin, currentMax)
}
```

To summarize, the minMax(array:) function returns a tuple containing two Int values. These values are called min and max so that they can be accessed by name when calling the function's return value. The body of the minMax(array:) function starts by assigning two working variables called current in and currentMax to the value of the first integer in the array. The function then iterates over the remaining values in the array and checks each value to examine if it is smaller or larger than the values of current in and currentMax. Normally, the overall minimum and maximum values are returned as a tuple of two Int values.

---

[6] https://docs.swift.org/swift-book/LanguageGuide/Functions.html, Swift

Because the tuple's member values are named as part of the function's return type, they can be accessed with dot syntax to retrieve the minimum and maximum found values:

```
let bounds = minMax(array: [8, -6, 2, 109,
3, 71])
print("min is \(bounds.min) and max is
\(bounds.max)")
// Prints "min is -6 and max is 109"
```

At the same time, keep in mind that the tuple's members do not need to be named at the point that the tuple is returned from the function, because their names are already viewed as a component of the function's return type.

Optional Tuple Return Types

In case the tuple type to be returned from a function can have "no value" for the entire tuple, you can use an optional tuple return type to state that the entire tuple can be nil. To do that, you write an optional tuple return type by adding a question mark after the tuple type's closing parenthesis, such as (Int, Int)? or (String, Int, Bool)?

An optional tuple type such as (Int, Int)? differs from a tuple that has optional types such as (Int?, Int?). With an optional tuple type, the entire tuple becomes optional, not just each individual value within the tuple. For instance, the minMax(array:) function above returns a tuple holding two Int values. However, the function does not complete any safety checks on the array it has passed. In case the array argument has an empty array, the minMax(array:) function, as described above, will trigger a runtime error when attempting to access array[0].

In order to manage an empty array safely, script the minMax(array:) function with an optional tuple return type and return a value of nil when the array is empty:[7]

```swift
func minMax(array: [Int]) -> (min: Int,
max: Int)? {
    if array.isEmpty {return nil}
    var currentMin = array[0]
    var currentMax = array[0]
    for value in array[1..<array.count] {
        if value < currentMin {
            currentMin = value
        } else if value > currentMax {
            currentMax = value
        }
    }
    return (currentMin, currentMax)
}
```

You can also use optional binding to see whether this version of the minMax(array:) function returns an actual tuple value or nil:

```swift
if let bounds = minMax(array: [8, -6, 2,
109, 3, 71]) {
    print("min is \(bounds.min) and max is
\(bounds.max)")
}
// Prints "min is -6 and max is 109"
```

---

[7] https://docs.swift.org/swift-book/LanguageGuide/Functions.html, Swift

Functions with an Implicit Return

When the entire body of the function comes as a single expression, the function ends up returning that expression. For example, both functions below have similar behavior:

```swift
func greeting(for person: String) -> String
{
    "Hello, " + person + "!"
}
print(greeting(for: "Dave"))
// Prints "Hello, David!"

func anotherGreeting(for person: String)
-> String {
    return "Hello, " + person + "!"
}
print(anotherGreeting(for: "David"))
// Prints "Hello, David!"
```

The entire definition of the greeting(for:) function is the greeting note that it returns, which means it can use this shorter form. The anotherGreeting(for:) function returns the same greeting message, using the return keyword like a longer function.

Function Argument Labels and Parameter Names

Every function parameter consists of both an argument label and a parameter name. The argument label is used for calling the function; each argument is written in the function call with its argument label before it. The parameter name is used when implementing the function.

By default, parameters apply their parameter name as their argument label:

```
func someFunction(firstParameterName: Int,
secondParameterName: Int) {
    // In the function body,
firstParameterName and secondParameterName
    // refer to the argument values for
the first and second parameters.
}
someFunction(firstParameterName: 1,
secondParameterName: 2)
```

In addition, all parameters should have unique names. Although it is possible for multiple parameters to use the same argument label, unique argument labels tend to make your code more readable.

It is also acceptable to define a default value for any parameter in a function by assigning a value to the parameter after that parameter's type. In case a default value is defined, you can skip that parameter when calling the function:

```
func someFunction(parameterWithoutDefault:
Int, parameterWithDefault: Int = 12) {
    // If you omit the second argument
when calling this function, then
    // the value of parameterWithDefault
is 12 inside the function body.
}
```

```
someFunction(parameterWithoutDefault: 3,
parameterWithDefault: 6) //
parameterWithDefault is 6
someFunction(parameterWithoutDefault: 4)
// parameterWithDefault is 12
```

It is recommended to place parameters that do not have default values at the beginning of a function's parameter list, before the parameters that have default values. Parameters[8] that do not have default values are treated as more important to the function's meaning—writing them first makes it easier to recognize that the same function is being called, regardless of whether any default parameters are omitted.

Variadic Parameters

A variadic is the parameter that accepts zero or more values of a particular type. You use a variadic parameter to indicate that the parameter can be passed a varying number of input values when the function is activated. Script variadic parameters by including three-period characters (…) after the parameter's type name.

The values added to a variadic parameter are made available within the function's body as an array of the suitable type. For instance, a variadic parameter with the name of numbers and a type of Double will be made available within the function's body as a constant array.

---

[8] https://docs.swift.org/swift-book/LanguageGuide/Functions.html, Swift

The example below examine the arithmetic mean for a list of numbers of any length:

```
func arithmeticMean(_ numbers: Double...) ->
Double {
    var total: Double = 0
    for number in numbers {
        total += number
    }
    return total / Double(numbers.count)
}
arithmeticMean(1, 2, 3, 4, 5)
// returns 3.0, which is the arithmetic
mean of these five numbers
arithmeticMean(3, 8.25, 18.75)
// returns 10.0, which is the arithmetic
mean of these three numbers
```

As you can observe, a function is allowed to have multiple variadic parameters. The first parameter that comes after a variadic parameter should have an argument label. The argument label makes it unambiguous which arguments are forwarded to the variadic parameter and which arguments are assigned to the parameters that come after the variadic parameter.

In-Out Parameters
By default, function parameters are treated as constants. Attempting to modify the value of a function parameter from within the body of that function can end up causing a compile-time error. This means that you cannot change the value of a parameter by mistake. If you need a function

to modify a parameter's value, and you want those changes to remain after the function call has ended, identify that parameter as an in-out parameter instead.

You can write an in-out parameter by placing the input keyword right before a parameter's type. An in-out parameter has a value that is offered to the function, is changed by the function, and is brought back out of the function to remove the original value. You can only pass a variable as the argument for an in-out parameter. It is not possible to pass a constant or a literal value as the argument because constants and literals cannot be edited. In another case, you can place an ampersand (&) directly before a variable's name when you pass it as an argument to an in-out parameter, to mark that it can be modified by the function.

Nested Functions

All of the functions we have reviewed so far in this chapter have been examples of global functions, which are defined at global scope. Additionally, you can also define functions inside the bodies of other functions, named nested functions.

Nested functions are mostly unrevealed to the outside world but can still be called and used by their enclosing function. An enclosing function can also return one of its nested functions to authorize the nested function to be used in another scope:

```
func chooseStepFunction(backward: Bool) ->
(Int) -> Int {
    func stepForward(input: Int) -> Int
{return input + 1}
```

```
    func stepBackward(input: Int) -> Int
{return input - 1}
    return backward? stepBackward:
stepForward
}
var currentValue = -4
let moveNearerToZero =
chooseStepFunction(backward: currentValue
> 0)
// moveNearerToZero now refers to the
nested stepForward() function
while currentValue != 0 {
    print("\(currentValue)… ")
    currentValue =
moveNearerToZero(currentValue)
}
print("zero!")
// -4…
// -3…
// -2…
// -1…
// zero!
```

OBJECTS AND CLASSES

Before getting in-depth about classes and structures, it is important to clarify a few commonly used terms in object-oriented programming. The terms classes, objects, and instances tend to confuse people new to object-oriented programming. Therefore, it is important that you know how Swift applies these terms. An instance of a class is traditionally known as an object. Yet Swift structures and classes are much closer in functionality than in other languages, and much of this chapter deals with functionality that applies to instances of either a class or a structure type.

Structures and classes could be defined as general-purpose, flexible constructs that act as the building blocks of your program's code. You define properties and methods to add functionality to your structures and classes using the same syntax you use to define constants, variables, and functions.

Unlike other programming languages, Swift does not require you to maintain separate interface and implementation files for custom structures and classes. In Swift, you keep a structure or class in a single file, and the external interface to that class or structure is automatically made available for other code to access.

Comparing Structures and Classes

Structures and classes in Swift have many features in common. Both have the capacity to:

- determine properties to store values,

- determine methods to ensure the functionality,

- define subscripts to enable access to their values using subscript syntax,

- define initializers to administer their initial state,

- stay extended to expand their functionality beyond a default implementation, and

- conform to protocols to maintain standard functionality of a certain kind.

At the same time, classes have certain additional capabilities that structures do not have:

- Inheritance allows one class to inherit the characteristics of another.

- Type casting lets you check and interpret the type of a class instance at runtime.

- Deinitializers enable an instance of a class to free any resources it has assigned.

- Reference counting assigns more than one reference to a class instance.

Nevertheless, structures and classes have a similar definition syntax. You can introduce structures with the struct keyword and classes with the class keyword. Both put their entire definition within a pair of braces:

```
struct SomeStructure {
    // structure definition goes here
}
class SomeClass {
    //class definition goes here
}
```

Every time you define a new structure or class, you define a new Swift type. Make sure to give types UpperCamelCase names (such as SomeStructure and SomeClass here) to match the capitalization of standard Swift types (such as String, Int, and Bool). Additionally, give properties and methods lowerCamelCase names (such as frameRate and incrementCount) to differentiate them from type names. To illustrate it with an example of a structure definition and a class definition:

```
struct Resolution {
    var width = 0
    var height = 0
}
class VideoMode {
    var resolution = Resolution()
    var interlaced = false
    var frameRate = 0.0
    var name: String?
}
```

You can see how the example above defines a new structure called Resolution, to identify a pixel-based display resolution. This structure has two stored properties called width and height. Stored properties are constants or variables that are combined and stored as part of the structure or class.

The example above also defines a new class called VideoMode, used to set a specific video mode for video display. This class has four variable stored properties. The first, resolution, is activated with a new Resolution structure instance, which infers a property type of Resolution. For the other three properties, new VideoMode instances will be initialized with an interlaced setting of false (or "noninterlaced video"), a playback frame rate of 0.0, and an optional String value called name. The name property is automatically assigned a default value of nil, or "no name value", because it is of an optional type.

Structure and Class Instances

The Resolution structure definition and the VideoMode class definition only state what a Resolution or VideoMode might look like. They cannot describe a specific resolution or video mode because in order to do that, you need to create an instance of the structure or class.

The syntax for creating such instances is very similar for both structures and classes:

```
let someResolution = Resolution()
let someVideoMode = VideoMode()
```

Structures and classes both use initializer syntax for new instances. The simplest form of initializer syntax uses the type name of the class or structure followed by empty parentheses, such as Resolution() or VideoMode(). This results in a new instance of the class or structure, with any properties initialized to their default values.

It is possible to access the properties of an instance using dot syntax. In dot syntax, you include the property name right after the instance name, separated by a period (.), without any spaces:

```
print("The width of someResolution is
\(someResolution.width)")
// Prints "The width of someResolution
is 0"
```

In this example, someResolution.width addresses to the width property of someResolution, and returns its default initial value of 0.

Alternatively, you can even refer to subproperties, such as the width property in the resolution property of a VideoMode:

```
print("The width of someVideoMode is
\(someVideoMode.resolution.width)")
// Prints "The width of someVideoMode is 0"
```

Or use dot syntax to assign a new value to a variable property:

```
someVideoMode.resolution.width = 1000
print("The width of someVideoMode is now
\(someVideoMode.resolution.width)")
// Prints "The width of someVideoMode is
now 1000"
```

Memberwise Initializers for Structure Types

All structures naturally have an automatically generated memberwise initializer, which you can apply to initialize the member properties of new structure instances. Initial values for the properties of the new instance can be passed to the memberwise initializer by name:

```
let VGA = Resolution(width: 60, height: 40)
```

Keep in mind that, unlike structures, class instances do not receive a default memberwise initializer.

Identity Operators

Since classes are reference types, it is possible for multiple constants and variables to refer to the same single instance of a class behind the scenes. The same, however, is not true for structures and enumerations, because they are copied when they are assigned to a constant or variable, or passed to a function.

Therefore, it can sometimes be useful to check whether two constants or variables refer to exactly the same instance of a class. To enable this, you can apply the following Swift identity operators:

- Identical to (===)

- Not identical to (!==)

You can use these operators to see whether two constants or variables refer to the same single instance:

```
if tenEighty === alsoTenEighty {
    print("tenEighty and alsoTenEighty
refer to the same VideoMode instance.")
}
//Prints "tenEighty and alsoTenEighty refer
to the same VideoMode instance."
```

Also important to understand that identical to does not mean the same thing as equal to. Identical to means that two constants or variables of class type refer to exactly the same class instance. Equal to means that two instances are treated as equal or equivalent in value, for some appropriate meaning of equal, as set by the type's designer.

Pointers

In case you have some previous experience with C, C++, or Objective-C, you may know that these languages add pointers to refer to addresses in memory. A Swift constant or variable that refers to an instance of some reference type is similar to a pointer in C but is not a direct pointer to an address in memory, and does not require you to write an asterisk (*) to mark that you are creating a reference. Instead, these references are stated like any other constant or variable in Swift. The standard library offers pointer and buffer types that you can apply if you need to interact with pointers directly.

ENUMERATIONS

An enumeration is used to define a common type for a group of connected values and enables you to administer those values in a type-safe manner within your code. In C language, enumerations assign related names to a set of integer values. Enumerations in Swift are more versatile and do not have to provide a value for each case of the enumeration. If a value (also known as a raw value) is provided for each enumeration case, the value could be a string, a character, or a value of any integer or floating-point type.

Alternatively, enumeration cases can explicitly determine values of any type to be placed along with each different case value, as unions or variants do in other languages. You can identify a common set of related cases as part of one enumeration, each of which has a different set of values of appropriate types that go with it.

Enumerations in Swift are often treated as first-class types in their own right. Meaning that they can adopt many features traditionally supported only by classes, like computed properties to provide additional information about the enumeration's current value, and instance methods to enable functionality related to the values the enumeration represents. Enumerations can also activate initializers to provide an initial case value. Moreover, they can be extended to expand their functionality beyond their original implementation and follow protocols to provide standard operability.

You introduce enumerations with the enum keyword and insert their entire definition within a pair of braces:

```
enum SomeEnumeration {
    // enumeration definition goes here
}
```

Let us take a look at this example with the four main points of a compass:[9]

```
enum CompassPoint {
    case north
    case south
    case east
    case west
}
```

The values defined in an enumeration (north, south, east, and west) are its enumeration cases. As you could observe, Swift enumeration cases do not have an integer value set by default, and in the CompassPoint example above, north, south, east and west do not precisely equal 0, 1, 2, and 3. Instead, the different enumeration cases are values in their own right, with an explicitly set type of CompassPoint.

---

[9] https://docs.swift.org/swift-book/LanguageGuide/Enumerations.html, Swift

You can also create multiple cases that appear on a single line, separated by commas:

```
enum Months {
    case january, february, march, april,
may, june, july, august
}
```

Each enumeration definition defines a new type. Similar to other types in Swift, their names (such as CompassPoint and Months) start with a capital letter. In addition, you can give enumeration types singular rather than plural names, so that they read as self-evident:

```
var directionToHead = CompassPoint.west
```

The type of directionToHead is combined when it is initialized with one of the possible values of CompassPoint. Once directionToHead is stated as a CompassPoint, you can assign it to a different CompassPoint value using shorter dot syntax:

```
directionToHead = .east
```

The type of directionToHead is already established, meaning that you can drop the type when setting its value. This makes for highly readable code when operating explicitly typed enumeration values.

Iterating over Enumeration Cases

For some enumerations, it is useful to have a library of all of that enumeration's cases. You enable this by including: CaseIterable after the enumeration's name and wait for

Swift to display a collection of all the cases as an allCases property of the enumeration type. To illustrate with an example:

```
enum Fastfood: CaseIterable {
    case pizza, burger, fries
}
let numberOfChoices = Fastfood.allCases.
count
print("\(numberOfChoices) fastfoods
available")
// Prints "3 fastfoods available"
```

In the example above, you write Fastfoods.allCases to access a collection that hold all of the cases of the Beverage enumeration. You can use allCases like any other collection—the collection's items are instances of the enumeration type, so in this case, they are Fastfood values.

Associated Values

The examples in the previous section present how the cases of an enumeration are a defined value in their own right. It is possible to set a constant or variable to Months.january and check for this value later. However, it might be useful to store values of other types alongside these case values. This additional data is called an associated value, and it varies each time you use that case as a value in your code.

You can apply Swift enumerations to store associated values of any given type, and the value types can be different for each case of the enumeration. Enumerations could also be called discriminated unions, tagged unions, or variants in other programming languages.

Raw Values

Associated Values show how cases of an enumeration can declare that they store associated values of different types. As an alternative to associated values, enumeration cases can come with default values or raw values, which are all of the same types. Here is an example that puts raw ASCII values alongside named enumeration cases:

```
enum ASCIIControlCharacter: Character {
    case tab = "\t"
    case lineFeed = "\n"
    case carriageReturn = "\r"
}
```

Here, the raw values for an enumeration called ASCIIControlCharacter are defined as the Character and are set to some of the more common ASCII control characters. Raw values can be strings, characters, or any of the integer or floating-point number types with each raw value unique within its enumeration declaration.

At the same time, raw values are not the same as associated values. Raw values are set to prepopulated values when you first identify the enumeration in your code. And associated values are set when you create a new constant or variable based on one of the enumeration's cases.

Implicitly Assigned Raw Values

When you are managing enumerations that store integer or string raw values, there is no need to explicitly assign a raw value for each case because Swift will automatically assign those values for you. For instance, when integers are used for raw values, the implicit value for each case is one more than the previous case. If the first case does not have a value set, its value is 0.

The enumeration below is a refinement of the earlier Months enumeration, with integer raw values to represent each month's order:

```
enum Month: Int {
    case january = 1, february, march,
april, may, june, july, august
}
```

In the example above, Month.january has an explicit raw value of 1, Month.february has an implicit raw value of 2, and so on.

When strings are used for raw values, the implicit value for each case is the text of that case's name. The enumeration below is a refinement of the earlier CompassPoint enumeration, with string raw values to represent each direction's name:

```
enum CompassPoint: String {
    case north, south, east, west
}
```

In the example above, CompassPoint.south has an implicit raw value of "south", and so on. You can access the raw value of an enumeration case using its rawValue property:

```
let marchOrder = Month.march.rawValue
// monthsOrder is 3

let sunsetDirection = CompassPoint.west.
rawValue
// sunsetDirection is "west"
```

Recursive Enumerations

A recursive enumeration is an enumeration that holds another instance of the enumeration as the associated value for one or more of the enumeration cases. You set the enumeration case as recursive by writing indirect before it, which tells the compiler to add the necessary layer of indirection. For instance, here an enumeration that stores simple arithmetic expressions:

```
enum ArithmeticExpression {
    case number(Int)
    indirect case
addition(ArithmeticExpression,
ArithmeticExpression)
    indirect case multiplication(Arithmeti
cExpression, ArithmeticExpression)
}
```

One can observe that this enumeration stores three kinds of arithmetic expressions: A plain number, the addition of two expressions, and the multiplication of two expressions. The addition and multiplication cases have assigned values that are also arithmetic expressions—these associated values leave space to create nest expressions. For example, the expression (5 + 4) * 2 has a number on the right-hand side of the multiplication and another expression on the left-hand side of the multiplication. Because the data is nested, the enumeration applied to store the data also needs to support nesting—this means the enumeration has to be recursive.

To summarize this chapter, we described Swift variables, constants, and learned about objects and classes. We also discussed how can one use and modify enumerations and functions to write sample projects with source code. The next chapter will complete the Swift toolset by learning about fetching data with URLSession and comparing dates with foundation. We shall also review some of the most useful techniques when working with JSON and XML.

CHAPTER 4

Swift Standard Library

IN THIS CHAPTER

➤ Reviewing Swift standard library items

➤ Learning how to deal with various library frameworks

➤ Working with JSON and XML in Swift

Most programming languages come with some form of the standard library that includes built-in, commonly used items of functionality, and Swift is no exception. At the same time, Swift takes the concept of a standard library even further, since much of the functionality that we typically consider to be features integrated into the language itself are actually executed within the standard library.

DOI: 10.1201/9781003254089-4

In the preceding chapter, we mainly covered Swift Basic Syntax, in this chapter we are going to learn new tips and tricks that can help you make the most of many of the features and Application Programming Interfaces (APIs) that the standard library offers—which in turn can contribute to the improvement of the speed, quality, and compatibility of the code that you write.

The Swift library provides higher-level functionality with powerful tools that developers can depend upon across all the platforms that Swift supports. The Core Libraries have a goal of providing stable and useful features in the following key areas:[1]

- Unit testing

- Networking primitives

- Scheduling and execution of work, including threads, queues, and notifications

- Persistence, including property lists, archives, JSON parsing, and XML parsing

- Support for dates, times, and calendrical calculations

- Interaction with the file system

- Internationalization, including date and number formatting and language-specific resources

- User preferences

---

[1] https://swift.org/core-libraries/, Swift

The Swift standard library could also be viewed as the framework that contains the core components, tools, and types to help build your Swift apps. And before you start building your own custom data structures, it is important to understand the primary data structures that the Swift standard library already provides. We have already talked about Strings, Ints, Floats, and Bools in Chapter 2. In this chapter, we will focus on the other three main data structures that the standard library provides right out of the box: Array, Dictionary, and Set.

ARRAY

An array is a general-purpose, generic structure used for storing an ordered collection of items. You can create an array by using an array literal, which is a comma-separated list of values surrounded by square brackets. To illustrate with an example:

```
let people = ["Bob", "Sam", "Ryan"]
```

Swift defines arrays using protocols. Each of these protocols allows more capabilities on the array. For instance, an Array is a Sequence, which means that you can iterate through it at least once. It is also a Collection, meaning it can be traversed multiple times, non-modified, and it can be accessed using a subscript operator. An array is also a RandomAccessCollection, which offers guarantees about its efficiency.

The Swift Array is called a generic collection because it can operate with any type. In fact, most of the Swift standard library is built with generic code. As with any data structure, there are certain traits that you should be familiar with. The first one would be the notion of order.

Order

Components in an array are explicitly ordered. Using the above people array as an example, "Bob" comes before "Sam." All items in an array have a corresponding zero-based, integer index. For instance, the people array from the above example has three indices, one corresponding to each component. You can retrieve the value of a component in the array by writing the following:

```
people[0]  //  "Bob"
people[1]  //  "Sam"
people[2]  //  "Ryan"
```

Order is determined by the array data structure and should not be taken for granted. Because there are other data structures, such as Dictionary, that have a weaker concept of order.

Random Access

Random access is another trait that data structures can claim if they can administer element retrieval in a constant amount of time. For example, getting "Ryan" from the people array takes constant time. Again, this performance should not be taken for granted since other data structures such as linked lists and trees do not have constant time access.

Apart from being a random-access collection, there are other areas of performance that you need to get to know. Particularly, what constitutes the data structure fare when the amount of data it contains needs to grow? For arrays, this varies on two factors.

The first factor is one in which you decide to insert the new element inside the array. The most basic scenario for adding an element to an array is to place it at the end of the array:

```
people.append("Charles")
print(people) // prints ["Bob", "Sam",
"Ryan", "Charles"]
```

Inserting "Charles" using the append method will put the string at the end of the array. This is a constant-time operation, meaning the time it takes to complete this operation stays the same no matter how large the array gets. Nevertheless, there may be a time when you need to insert an element in a particular location, such as in the very middle of the array. And in general, inserting new element from anywhere aside from the end of the array will force components to shuffle backward to make space for the new item:

```
people.insert("Andy", at: 0)
// ["Andy", "Bob", "Sam", "Ryan", "Charles"]
```

To put it simply, every element should shift backward by one index. In case the number of elements in the array doubles, the time required for this insert operation will also double. If inserting elements in front of a collection is a common operation for your program, you might want to consider a different data structure to contain your data.

The second factor that regulates the speed of insertion is the array's capacity. Swift arrays are allocated with a predetermined amount of space for its components. If you try to include new elements to an array that is already at maximum capacity, the Array would completely restructure itself to make more room for more elements. This is done by copying all the current elements of the array in a new and bigger container in memory. Yet by deciding on this, be prepared that it might take time as each element of the array would be separately reviewed and copied.

Dictionary

A dictionary is another generic collection that consists of key-value pairs. To demonstrate, here is a dictionary containing a user's name and a score:

```
var scores: [String: Int] = ["Eric": 9,
"Mark": 12, "Wayne": 1]
```

Dictionaries do not come with guarantees of order, nor can you insert at a specific index. They also put a requirement on the Key type that it be Hashable, meaning its value will not change during its lifetime. Yet since almost all of the standard types are already Hashable in the more recent versions of Swift, adopting the Hashable protocol is not necessary. You can add a new entry to the dictionary with the following syntax:

```
scores["Ashton"] = 0
```

This creates a new key-value pair in the dictionary:

```
["Eric": 9, "Mark": 12, "Ashton": 0,
"Wayne": 1]
```

The "Ashton" key is included somewhere in the dictionary. Dictionaries are unordered, so you cannot guarantee where new entries will be located.

It is possible to traverse through the key-values of a dictionary multiple times as the Collection protocol affords. This order, even if undefined, will be the same every time it is traversed until the collection is modified. The lack of ordering capacity comes with some redeeming traits. Unlike the array, dictionaries do not need to worry about elements shifting around. Inserting into a dictionary always takes a fixed amount of time. Lookup operations also take a constant amount of time, which is significantly faster than searching for a particular element in an array which requires a walk from the beginning of the array to the insertion point.

Set

A set is a data structure that consists of unique values. You can think of it as a bag that allows you to put items into it, but rejects items that have already been inserted:

```
var bag: Set<String> = ["Cake", "Juice",
"Candy"]
bag.insert("Cake")
print(bag) // prints ["Cake", "Juice",
"Candy"]
```

Since sets promote uniqueness, they lend themselves to a variety of interesting applications, such as searching for duplicate items in a collection of values:

```
let values: [String] = [...]
var bag: Set<String> = []
for value in values {
  if bag.contains(value) {
    // bag already has it, therefore, it
is a duplicate
  }
  bag.insert(value)
}
```

Although you probably will not use sets nearly as much as arrays and dictionaries, it is still common enough to be a key data structure to keep in your toolbelt. There is one disadvantage to sets though—similar to dictionaries, values in a set do not have a notion of order. Keep that in mind when you use a set to go through your data.

To summarize this section:

- Every data structure has advantages and disadvantages. Knowing them is important to writing performant software.

- Functions such as insert(at:) for Array have performance characteristics that can mess performance when used randomly. If you need to use insert(at:) frequently with indices near the beginning of the array, you should consider using a different data structure such as the linked list.

- Dictionary trades away the ability to keep the order of its elements for fast insertion and searching.

- Set guarantees uniqueness in a collection of values, but on the other hand, it abandons the ability to maintain the order of the elements.

COMPARING DATES WITH FOUNDATION

The Swift library could be defined as a base layer of functionality that is required for almost all applications. It offers primitive classes and introduces key paradigms that constitute functionality not provided by the language or runtime. It is created with these goals in mind:

- To provide a set of basic utility classes

- To make software development easier by including consistent conventions

- To support internationalization and localization by making software accessible to users around the world

- To provide a level of OS independence, to enhance portability

The Swift makes use of many underlying libraries as Apple's programming language but has been built to be completely independent of the Objective-C runtime. Because of this, it might look like a substantial reimplementation of the same API, using pure Swift code layered on top of these common underlying libraries.

Libraries that we are going to review are part of our ongoing work to extend the cross-platform capabilities of Swift.

They were made part of the open-source release so that everyone can work on them together with the community. In this section, we will look through three existing Swift libraries: libdispatch, XCTest, and mainly, the Foundation.

libdispatch

Grand Central Dispatch (GCD or libdispatch) is a library set to provide comprehensive support for concurrent code execution on multicore hardware.

libdispatch is currently ongoing renovation as Swift is aiming to incorporate as much of the portable subset of the API as possible to it, using the existing open-source C execution.

XCTest

The XCTest library is established to provide a common framework for writing unit tests in Swift, for Swift packages and applications. XCTest uses the same API as the XCTest you might be familiar with from Xcode. Thus, you can use the XCTest framework to script unit tests for your Xcode projects that integrate seamlessly with Xcode's testing workflow.

Tests assert that certain requirements are met during code execution, and record test failures if those conditions are not satisfied. Tests can also estimate the performance of blocks of code to see for any performance regressions and can interact with an application's user interface (UI) to verify user interaction flows.

Foundation

This framework provides a basic foundation of functionality for apps and frameworks, including data storage, text processing, date and time calculations, sorting and filtering, and networking. The classes, protocols, and data types used by Foundation are similar for the macOS, iOS, watchOS, and tvOS software development kit (SDKs).

Naturally, Foundation supports two approaches for data formatting:

When operating in Swift, you can apply formatted methods directly on the types you need to format, optionally using FormatStyle and its subtypes to customize formatter output. This approach supports dates, integers, floating-point numbers, measurements, sequences, and person name components. Foundation caches identically-configured formatter instances internally, allowing you to focus on your app's formatting needs.

The second approach is creating instances of Formatter and its subtypes, using the string(for:) method to convert objects to formatted strings. The following is the list of available formatters:[2]

- **For Numbers and Currency**

  - **class NumberFormatter:** A formatter that converts between numeric values and their textual representations.

- **For Names**

  - **class PersonNameComponentsFormatter:** A formatter that provides localized representations of the components of a person's name

---

[2] https://developer.apple.com/documentation/foundation/data_formatting, Apple

- **For Dates and Times**

  - **class DateFormatter:** A formatter that converts between dates and their textual representations

  - **class DateComponentsFormatter:** A formatter that creates string representations of quantities of time

  - **class RelativeDateTimeFormatter:** A formatter that creates locale-aware string representations of a relative date or time

  - **class DateIntervalFormatter:** A formatter that creates string representations of time intervals

  - **class ISO8601DateFormatter:** A formatter that converts between dates and their string representations

- **For Data Sizes**

  - **class ByteCountFormatter:** A formatter that converts a byte count value into a localized description that is formatted with the appropriate byte modifier

- **For Measurements**

  - **class MeasurementFormatter:** A formatter that provides localized representations of units and measurements

- **For Lists**

  - **class ListFormatter:** An object that provides locale-correct formatting of a list of items using the appropriate separator and conjunction

Now, let us look at the date structure and its options in detail. Fundamentally, data structure provides methods for comparing dates, calculating the time interval between two dates, and creating a new date from a time interval relative to another date. A basic date value stands for a single point in time, independent of any particular calendrical system or time zone. Date values represent a time interval relative to an absolute reference date. You can use date values together with DateFormatter instances to create localized representations of dates and times and with Calendar instances to complete calendar arithmetic. The following is the list of available date instances:[3]

- **Creating a Date**

  - **init():** Creates a date value initialized to the current date and time

  - **init(timeIntervalSinceNow: TimeInterval):** Creates a date value initialized relative to the current date and time by a given number of seconds

  - **init(timeInterval: TimeInterval, since: Date):** Creates a date value initialized relative to another given date by a given number of seconds

  - **init(timeIntervalSinceReferenceDate: Time-Interval):** Creates a date value initialized relative to 00:00:00 Coordinated Universal Time (UTC) on January 1, 2000 by a given number of seconds

---

[3] https://developer.apple.com/documentation/foundation/dates_and_times, Apple

- **init(timeIntervalSince1970: TimeInterval):** Creates a date value initialized relative to 00:00:00 UTC on January 1, 1970, by a given number of seconds

- **init(from: Decoder):** Creates a new instance by decoding from the given decoder

- **Getting Temporal Boundaries**

  - **static let distantFuture: Date:** A date value representing a date in the distant future

  - **static let distantPast: Date:** A date value representing a date in the distant past

- **Comparing Dates**

  - **static func == (Date, Date) -> Bool:** Returns a Boolean value that indicates whether two dates represent the same point in time

  - **static func != (Date, Date) -> Bool:** Returns a Boolean value that indicates whether two dates don't represent the same point in time

  - **static func > (Date, Date) -> Bool:** Returns a Boolean value that indicates whether the value of the first argument is greater than that of the second argument

  - **static func >= (Date, Date) -> Bool:** Returns a Boolean value indicating whether the value of the first argument is greater than or equal to that of the second argument

- **static func < (Date, Date) -> Bool:** Returns a Boolean value that indicates whether the value of the first argument is less than that of the second argument

- **static func <= (Date, Date) -> Bool:** Returns a Boolean value indicating whether the value of the first argument is less than or equal to that of the second argument

- **func compare(Date) -> ComparisonResult:** Compares another date to this one

- **func distance(to: Date) -> TimeInterval:** Returns the distance from this date to another date, specified as a time interval

- **Getting Time Intervals**

  - **func timeIntervalSince(Date) -> TimeInterval:** Returns the interval between this date and another given date

  - **var timeIntervalSinceNow: TimeInterval:** The time interval between the date value and the current date and time

  - **var timeIntervalSinceReferenceDate: TimeInterval:** The interval between the date value and 00:00:00 UTC on January 1, 2001

  - **var timeIntervalSince1970: TimeInterval:** The interval between the date value and 00:00:00 UTC on January 1, 1970

- **static var timeIntervalSinceReferenceDate: TimeInterval:** The interval between 00:00:00 UTC on January 1, 2001 and the current date and time

- **static let timeIntervalBetween1970AndReferenceDate: Double:** The number of seconds from January 1, 1970 to the reference date, January 1, 2000

- **typealias Date.Stride:** A type alias to define the stride of a date

- **Adding or Subtracting a Time Interval**

  - **func addTimeInterval(TimeInterval):** Adds a time interval to this date

  - **func addingTimeInterval(TimeInterval) -> Date:** Creates a new date value by adding a time interval to this date

  - **func advanced(by: TimeInterval) -> Date:** Returns a date offset the specified time interval from this date

  - **static func + (Date, TimeInterval) -> Date:** Returns a date with a specified amount of time added to it

  - **static func += (inout Date, TimeInterval):** Adds a time interval to a date

  - **static func - (Date, TimeInterval) -> Date:** Returns a date with a specified amount of time subtracted from it

  - **static func -= (inout Date, TimeInterval):** Subtracts a time interval from a date

- **Creating Date Ranges**

  - **static func ... (Date) -> PartialRangeFrom<Date>:** Returns a partial range extending upward from a lower bound

  - **static func ... (Date) -> PartialRangeThrough-<Date>:** Returns a partial range up to, and including, its upper bound

  - **static func ... (Date, Date) -> ClosedRange<Date>:** Returns a closed range that contains both of its bounds

  - **static func ...< (Date) -> PartialRangeUpTo<Date>:** Returns a partial range up to, but not including, its upper bound

  - **static func ...< (Date, Date) -> Range<Date>:** Returns a half-open range that contains its lower bound but not its upper bound

- **Encoding Dates**

  - **func encode(to: Encoder):** Encodes this date into the given encoder

- **Describing Dates**

  - **var description: String:** A textual description of the date value

  - **func description(with: Locale?) -> String:** Returns a string representation of the date using the given locale

  - **var debugDescription: String:** A textual description of the date suitable for debugging

- **var customMirror: Mirror:** A mirror that reflects the date

- **var hashValue: Int:** The computed hash value of the date

- **func hash(into: inout Hasher):** Hashes the essential components of this value by feeding them into the given hasher

- **Using Reference Types**

  - **class NSDate:** A representation of a specific point in time, for use when you need reference semantics or other Foundation-specific behavior

  - **typealias Date.ReferenceType:** An alias for this value type's equivalent reference type

- **Date Representations**

  - **struct Date:** A specific point in time, independent of any calendar or time zone

  - **struct DateInterval:** The span of time between a specific start date and end date

  - **typealias TimeInterval:** A number of seconds

- **Calendrical Calculations**

  - **struct DateComponents:** A date or time specified in terms of units (such as year, month, day, hour, and minute) to be evaluated in a calendar system and time zone

- **struct Calendar:** A definition of the relationships between calendar units (such as eras, years, and weekdays) and absolute points in time, providing features for calculation and comparison of dates

- **struct TimeZone:** Information about standard time conventions associated with a specific geo-political region

- **Date Formatting**

  - **class DateFormatter:** A formatter that converts between dates and their textual representations

  - **class DateComponentsFormatter:** A formatter that creates string representations of quantities of time

  - **class DateIntervalFormatter:** A formatter that creates string representations of time intervals

  - **class ISO8601DateFormatter:** A formatter that converts between dates and their ISO 8601 string representations

- **Internationalization**

  - **struct Locale:** Information about linguistic, cultural, and technological conventions for use in formatting data for presentation

Creating a DateInterval Instance

As the name implies, a DateInterval instance stands for an interval between two dates. Even though the DateInterval structure is a relatively simple type, it abstracts the details of working with date intervals. This is reflected by one of the initializers the DateInterval structure defines, init(start:end:):

```
import Foundation
let now = Date()
let tomorrow = now.addingTimeInterval(24.0 *
3600.0)
let dateInterval = DateInterval(start:
now, end: tomorrow)
```

The DateInterval structure defines three basic initializers. We shall take a look at each of these initializers:

init(start:duration:)

The init(start:duration:) initializer of the DateInterval structure determines a start date and a duration of type TimeInterval. Because the start date of a date interval has to be earlier than the end date, the duration cannot be less than 0. An exception is thrown if you pass a negative duration to the initializer. To illustrate the initializer with an example:

```
import Foundation
let now = Date()
let dateInterval = DateInterval(start: now,
duration: 3.0 * 24.0 * 3600.0)
```

init(start:end:)

We already mentioned the init(start:end:) initializer that accepts a start date and an end date:

```
import Foundation
let now = Date()
```

```
let tomorrow = now.addingTimeInterval(24.0 *
3600.0)
let dateInterval = DateInterval(start:
now, end: tomorrow)
```

The same timing rule applies to this initializer as well—if the start date is later than the end date, an exception is thrown.

init()

If you create a DateInterval instance by invoking init(), the startDate and endDate properties would be equal. This also means that the value of the duration property would be 0.

Properties

It has already been mentioned that the DateInterval structure is a very straightforward, lightweight type. It defines three main properties:

1. start of type Date

2. end of type Date

3. and duration of type TimeInterval

Operations

What makes the DateInterval structure interesting is the range of operations you can perform on DateInterval instances. Not only can you compare date intervals, but you can also regulate intersections, or you can ask an instance whether it contains a particular date.

Generally, date operations could look unordered and therefore prone to errors. The DateInterval structure makes this less of a problem.

One of the most widely used DateInterval structure is the intersection(with:) method. This method accepts another date interval and returns the intersection of the date intervals. To illustrate with an example:[4]

```
import Foundation
let start1 = Date(timeIntervalSinceNow:
-470482.0)
let end1 = Date(timeIntervalSinceNow:
20482.0)

let start2 = start1.
addingTimeInterval(112560.0)
let end2 = end1.
addingTimeInterval(-222304.0)

let dateInterval1 = DateInterval(start:
start1, end: end1)
let dateInterval2 = DateInterval(start:
start2, end: end2)

let intersection = dateInterval1.
intersection(with: dateInterval2)
```

The DateIntervalFormatter class has been around since iOS 8 and macOS 10.10. In addition, Apple included a

---

[4] https://cocoacasts.com/working-with-nsdateinterval-in-swift, Cocoacasts

convenience method in iOS 10 and macOS 10.12 to add support for the DateInterval structure. This is how it runs:

```
import Foundation
let start1 = Date(timeIntervalSinceNow:
-470482.0)
let end1 = Date(timeIntervalSinceNow:
20482.0)

let start2 = start1.
addingTimeInterval(112560.0)
let end2 = end1.
addingTimeInterval(-222304.0)

let dateInterval1 = DateInterval(start:
start1, end: end1)
let dateInterval2 = DateInterval(start:
start2, end: end2)

let intersection = dateInterval1.
intersection(with: dateInterval2)

if let intersection = dateInterval1.
intersection(with: dateInterval2) {
    // Initialize Date Interval Formatter
    let dateIntervalFormatter =
DateIntervalFormatter()

    // Configure Date Interval Formatter
    dateIntervalFormatter.dateStyle =
.short
    dateIntervalFormatter.timeStyle =
.medium
```

```
    // String From Date Interval
    dateIntervalFormatter.string(from:
intersection)
}
```

As one can observe, you initialize an instance of the DateIntervalFormatter class by specifying the date and time style, invoking the string(from:) method, and finally by passing in a DateInterval instance.

Overall, the Foundation framework is packed with a variety of classes, structures, and functions that can make your life as a developer easier. The DateInterval structure is one such type within the framework.

FETCHING DATA WITH URLSESSION

Fetching and downloading data from and to web services is a skill any starting iOS developer should master, and URLSession offers a first-party best-in-class API to make networking requests.

Since iOS 7, the most convenient way of making HTTP networking requests is by using a class called URLSession. The URLSession class is actually part of a set of classes that operate together to make and respond to HTTP requests.

The URL environment works in the following way:

- You use URLSession to create a session. You can think of a session as an open tab or window in the browser, which groups together many HTTP requests over subsequent website visits.

- The URLSession is used to create URLSessionTask instances, which can fetch and return data to your app, as well as download and upload files to web services.

- You configure a session with a URLSessionConfiguration object. This configuration manages caching, cookies, connectivity, and credentials.

- To make a request, you create a data task, of class URLSessionDataTask, and you provide it with a URL, such as https://twitter.com/api/, and a completion handler. This is a closure that is implemented when the request's response is returned to your app.

Additionally, you use a URLSession to make multiple subsequent requests, as URLSessionTask instances. A task always comes as part of a session. The URLSession could be seen as a factory that you use to set up and implement different URLSessionTasks, based on the parameters you set.

With URLSession, there are three types of tasks to consider:

- **Data tasks** send and receive data with URLSessionDataTask, by using NSData objects. They're the most common for web service requests, for instance when working with JSON.

- **Upload tasks** send files to a webserver with URLSessionUploadTask. They are similar to data tasks, but URLSessionUploadTask instances can also upload data in the background.

- **Download tasks** download files from a webserver with URLSessionDownloadTask by directly writing to a temporary file. You can observe the progress of file downloads, pause and resume them.

Fetching sample data with URLSession is going to consist of the following steps:

1. Setting up the HTTP request with URLSession

2. Making the request with URLSessionDataTask

3. Printing the returned response data

4. Validating the response data

5. Converting the response data to JSON

Setting Up the HTTP Request with URLSession

First, you should set up the request you want to make. As discussed before, you will need a URL and a session similar to this:

```
let session = URLSession.shared
let url = URL(string: "…")!
```

The URL we'll request is users.json (Right-click, then Copy Link).

In the above code, you are initializing a URL constant of type URL. The URLSession.shared singleton stands as a reference to a shared URLSession instance that has no configuration.

Making the Request with URLSessionDataTask

Next, you have to create a data task with the dataTask(with: completionHandler:) function of URLSession:

```
let task = session.dataTask(with: url,
completionHandler: {data, response, error in
    // Insert something…
})
```

A few things are noteworthy here. First, you should remember to assign the return value of dataTask(with:completion Handler:) to the task constant. The dataTask(with:comple tionHandler:) has two parameters: the request URL, and a completion handler. You have created that request URL earlier, so that is done. The completion handler is quite different. It is a closure that is activated when the request completes, so when a response has returned from the webserver. This can be any kind of response, including errors, timeouts, 404s, and actual JSON data.

The closure has three parameters: the response Data object, a URLResponse object, and an Error object. All of these closure parameters are optional, so they can be nil. At the same time, each of these parameters has its own specific purpose:

- You can use the data object, of type Data, to check out what data you got back from the webserver, such as the JSON you might have requested.

- The response object, of type URLResponse, is used to define the request's response, such as its length, encoding, HTTP status code, and return header fields.

- The error object contains an Error object if an error occurred while making the request. If no error occurred, it stays simply nil.

It is recommended to validate anything you get back: errors, expected HTTP status codes, malformed JSON, and so on. At this point, the network request has not been executed yet, it has only been set up. Here is how you start the request:

```
task.resume()
```

By calling the resume() function on the task object, the request is executed and the completion handler is activated.

Printing the Returned Response Data

The following code is what you actually get back once the completion handler activated:

```
let task = session.dataTask(with: url) {
data, response, error in
    print(data)
    print(response)
    print(error)
}
```

When the above code is executed, this is pointed out:

- The data value prints something like Optional(321 bytes). And since data is a Data object, so it has no visual representation yet. You can convert or interpret it as JSON, though, but that would require additional code.

- The response is of type NSHTTPURLResponse, a subclass of URLResponse, and it holds a ton of data about the response itself. The HTTP status code is 200, and from the HTTP headers, we can see that this request passed through Cloudflare.

Validating the Response Data

Now let us move to validation in the completion handler. When you're making HTTP networking requests, you are expected to validate whether any errors occur, check the HTTP response code and the correct data format.

First, in order to check if error is nil or not run the following:

```
if error != nil {
    // OH NO! An error occurred...
    self.handleClientError(error)
    return
}
```

Inside the error != nil conditional you can insert two of the following:

- Call a function that can deal with the response

- Throw an error with throw and use promises to deal with any thrown or passed errors in the chain's .catch clause

Then, to check if the HTTP status code is appropriate write the following:

```
guard let httpResponse = response as?
HTTPURLResponse,
      (200...299).contains(httpResponse.
statusCode) else {
    self.handleServerError(response)
    return
}
```

Here, the guard let syntax examine if the two conditions evaluate to false, and when that happens, the else clause is implemented. It literally "guards" that these two conditions are true. The first condition is an optional downcast from the response of type URLResponse to HTTPURLResponse. This downcast ensures you can apply the statusCode property on the response, which is only part of HTTPURLResponse.

The range (200…299) is a sequence of HTTP status codes that are regarded as suitable. Therefore, when status-Code is contained in 200…299, the response is regarded as correct. When it is not correct, for example, if you get a 500 Internal Server Error, the function handleServerError() is called.

The next validation you can do is to check the so-called MIME type of the response. This is a value that most web servers return, that explains what the format of the response data is. And since you are expecting JSON, so that is what you need to check:

```
guard let mime = response.mimeType, mime
== "application/JSON" else {
    print("Wrong MIME type!")
    return
}
```

The above code uses the same guard let syntax to make sure that response.mimeType equals application/JSON. In case it does not, you will need to respond appropriately and attempt to recover from the error.

Converting the Response Data to JSON

Let us imagine that the response from the above syntax is appropriate, meaning that now you can try and parse it to a JSON object in the following way:

```
if let json = try? JSONSerialization.
jsonObject(with: data!, options: []) {
    print(json)
}
```

And here is what is notable in the above code:

- You should apply the jsonObject(with:options:) function of the JSONSerialization class to serialize the data to JSON. Basically, the data is read character by character and turned into a JSON object so that you can easily read it.

- The optional binding with try? is an additional feature you can temporarily use to silence any errors from jsonObject(…). Errors can occur during serialization, and when they do, the return value of jsonObject(…) is nil, and the conditional stops running.

And while on it, here is the proper way to deal with any errors that shall occur:

```
do {
    let json = try JSONSerialization.
jsonObject(with: data!, options: [])
    print(json)
} catch {
    print("JSON error: \(error.
localizedDescription)")
}
```

As you can notice, errors thrown from the line marked with try are caught in the catch block. You could also have rethrown the error, and dealt with it in another part of the code.

In case the JSON data is correct, it is assigned to the json constant and printed out. And you can finally see that this is the response data from that URL you started with:

```
(
    {
        age = 5000;
        "first_name" = Matt;
        "last_name" = Ford;
    },
        {
        age = 999;
        "first_name" = Andrew;
        "last_name" = Bergman;
    },
        {
        age = 42;
        "first_name" = Arthur;
        "last_name" = Danton;
    },
        {
        age = 1234;
        "first_name" = Tristan;
        "last_name" = Perel;
    }
)
```

To sum up, here is the complete code we have written so far:[5]

```
let session = URLSession.shared
let url = URL(string: "…")!
```

---

[5] https://learnappmaking.com/urlsession-swift-networking-how-to/, Learnappmaking

```swift
let task = session.dataTask(with: url)
{data, response, error in
    if error != nil || data == nil {
        print("Client error!")
        return
    }
    guard let response = response as?
HTTPURLResponse, (200...299).
contains(response.statusCode) else {
        print("Server error!")
        return
    }
    guard let mime = response.mimeType,
mime == "application/json" else {
        print("Wrong MIME type!")
        return
    }
    do {
        let json = try JSONSerialization.
jsonObject(with: data!, options: [])
        print(json)
    } catch {
        print("JSON error: \(error.
localizedDescription)")
    }
}
task.resume()
```

In case you need to run the above code in Xcode Playground, it is smart to apply PlaygroundPage.current.needsIndefiniteExecution = true to enable infinite execution.

Making POST Requests with URLSession

Another standard task of HTTP networking is uploading data to a webserver, and specifically making so-called POST requests. Instead of fetching data from a web server, we are going to look at how to send data back to that webserver. A good example of such activity is logging into a website. Your username and password are sent to the webserver. And this webserver then checks your username and password against what's stored in the database and sends a response back. Similarly, when your Twitter app is used to create a new tweet, you send a POST request to the Twitter API with the tweet's text.

Here are the steps you should go through to accomplish such a task:

1. Start with setting up the HTTP POST request with URLSession

2. Set up the request headers and body

3. Make the request with URLSessionUploadTask

4. Print the returned response data

Setting Up the HTTP POST Request with URLSession

Making POST requests with URLSession mostly comes down to configuring the request. You can do this by adding some data to a URLRequest object:

```
let session = URLSession.shared
let url = URL(string: "https://example.
com/post")!

var request = URLRequest(url: url)
request.httpMethod = "POST"
```

With the above code, you are first creating a session constant with the shared URLSession instance, and setting up a URL object that refers to https://example.com/post. Then, with that URL object, you can create an instance of URLRequest and assign it to the request variable.

Setting Up the Request Headers and Body

You can also use the URLRequest object to set HTTP Headers. A header is a special parameter that is sent as part of the request, and it typically holds special information for the webserver or the web application. A good example is the Cookie header, which is used to send cookie information back and forth. You should start by adding a few headers to the request:

```
request.setValue("application/JSON",
forHTTPHeaderField: "Content-Type")
request.setValue("Powered by Swift!",
forHTTPHeaderField: "X-Powered-By")
```

Now, this request needs a body of some data, typically text, that is offered as part of the request message. In our case, it will be a JSON object that is delivered as a Data object. You should start by creating a simple dictionary with some values:

```
let json = [
    "username": "bedear42",
    "message": "Nice to meet you!"
]
```

Then, you need to turn that dictionary into a Data object with:

```
let jsonData = try! JSONSerialization.
data(withJSONObject: JSON, options: [])
```

The above step uses that same JSONSerialization class that we used before, but this time it does the exact opposite: turn an object into a Data object, that uses the JSON format.

Making the Request with URLSessionUploadTask

You can now send the jsonData to the webserver with a URLSessionUploadTask instance using the request and the data to create the task, instead of just the URL:

```
let task = session.uploadTask(with:
request, from: jsonData) {data, response,
error in
    // Do something…
}
task.resume()
```

With the above code, you are creating a task with session.uploadTask(…, and providing request and jsonData as parameters. Instead of creating a simple data task, the above request will include those headers, body, and URL we configured. Additionally, you can specify a completion handler, and the request is started once you call task.resume().

Printing the Returned Response Data

Inside the completion handler you are expected to validate the response by reading the response data with:

```
if let data = data, let dataString =
String(data: data, encoding: .utf8) {
    print(dataString)
}
```

The above code includes optional binding to turn the data optional into a String instance. And because the https:// example.com/post URL does not respond to POST requests, you might get the following error message in HTML format:

```
<?xml version="1.0" encoding="iso-8859-1"?>
<!DOCTYPE html PUBLIC "-//W3C//DTD XHTML
1.0 Transitional//EN"
     "http://www.w3.org/TR/xhtml1/DTD/
xhtml1-transitional.dtd">
<html xmlns="http://www.w3.org/1999/xhtml"
xml:lang="en" lang="en">
    <head>
        <title>404 - Not Found</title>
    </head>
    <body>
        <h1>404 - Not Found</h1>
        </body>
</html>
```

And with the following code you can see that the HTTP status code is actually 404 Not Found:

```
if let httpResponse = response as?
HTTPURLResponse {
    print(httpResponse.statusCode)
}
```

WORKING WITH JSON

When your app communicates with a web application, information returned from the server is often formatted as JSON. You can use the Foundation framework's JSONSerialization class to convert JSON into Swift data types like Dictionary, Array, String, Number, and Bool. However, because you cannot be certain of the structure or values of JSON your app receives, it can be challenging to deserialize model objects correctly. In this section, we shall describe a few approaches you can take when managing JSON in your apps.

Fundamentally, JSON stands for JavaScript Object Notation. JSON is a lightweight format for storing and transferring data. The JSON format contains a great variety of keys and values. You can think of this format as a dictionary where each key is unique, and the values can be strings, numbers, bools, or null. JSON can be stored as a multi-line String in Swift and converted to a Data object, and vice versa through the use of Decodable and Encodable protocols.

Below is a simple JSON object with two keys.

```
{
    "name": "John",
    "age": 20
}
```

Creating a Model

The first step to convert a JSON object to a Swift type is to create a model. For our example above, here is a struct you can use:

```
struct Person: Codable {
    var name: String
    var age: Int
}
```

As you can observe, each JSON key is represented by the property in the model above. You just have to make sure to conform to the Codable protocol so it can be used to decode and encode JSON.

Nested JSON Objects

You most certainly will be working with nested JSON objects as well. Here is a straightforward approach to managing this:

```
let person = """
{
    "name": "John",
    "age": 20,
    "birthplace": {
        "latitude": 37.3326,
        "longitude": 122.0055
    }
}
"""
struct Person: Codable {
    var name: String
    var age: Int
    var birthplace: Birthplace

    struct Birthplace: Codable {
        var latitude: Double
        var longitude: Double
    }
}
```

Decodable and Encodable Protocols

Swift has three protocols that make working with JSON simple—Decodable, Encodable, and Codable. Let us look at them one by one:

- **Encodable:** By defining your model type as Encodable, you tell Swift that you need to use this type to convert instances of Person to a JSON object. Most commonly this is applied to send data to the server.

- **Decodable:** By defining your model type as Decodable, you tell Swift that you need to use this type to convert JSON to Person instances. Most commonly this is used when receiving data from the server.

- **Codable:** Codable is a type alias for Decodable and Encodable which is done through Swift's protocol composition.

Whether you set your type as Encodable, Decode, or Codable, is up to you. Some may be required to be explicit with their naming and stick with the Encodable and Decodable; you may also simply mark the code as Codable unless told otherwise.

Coding Keys

The property naming convention in Swift is camelCase. There are a few examples of common naming conventions in programming:

- camelCase

- snake_case

- Pascal_Case

Some APIs will have keys formatted other than camelCase. To keep your code clean and follow the Swift convention, Swift offers a CodingKey protocol. This protocol regulates your program to use custom keys while keeping the camelCase convention. The convention is to create an enum named CodingKeys inside the type:

```
{
    "name": "John",
    "age": 20,
    "full_name_of_person": "John Smith"
}
struct Person: Codable {
    var name: String
    var age: Int
    var fullName: String

    enum CodingKeys: String, CodingKey {
        case name
        case age
        case fullName = "full_name_of_
person" //this string value should match
EXACTLY with the corresponding key in the
JSON object
    }
}
```

JSONDecoder and JSONEncoder

Swift has two classes for handling JSON—JSONDecoder and JSONEncoder:

JSONDecoder

Decoding allows Swift to convert a JSON object to a Swift type. Using the example from above, let us create an instance of JSONDecoder. Below are the steps to convert a JSON string to your Person type:[6]

```
let person = """
{
    "name": "John",
    "age": 20,
    "full_name": "John Smith"
}
"""
//1 - Create a model
struct Person: Codable {
    var name: String
    var age: Int
    var fullName: String
}


//2 - Convert the string to data
let personData = Data(person.utf8)


//3 - Create a JSONDecoder instance
let jsonDecoder = JSONDecoder()


//4 - set the keyDecodingStrategy to
convertFromSnakeCase on the jsonDecoder
instance
jsonDecoder.keyDecodingStrategy =
.convertFromSnakeCase
```

─────────────────
[6] https://medium.com/swlh/how-to-work-with-json-in-swift-83cd93a837e, Medium

```
//5 - Use the jsonDecoder instance to
decode the json into a Person object
do {
    let decodedPerson = try jsonDecoder.
decode(Person.self, from: personData)
    print("Person -- \(decodedPerson.name)
was decode and their age is:
\(decodedPerson.age)")
} catch {
    print("Error: \(error.
localizedDescription)")
}
```

JSONEncoder

Encoding allows Swift to convert a Swift type into a valid JSON object:

```
struct Person: Codable {
    var name: String
    var age: Int
}
let person = Person(name: "John", age: 20)

let jsonEncoder = JSONEncoder()
jsonEncoder.outputFormatting =
.prettyPrinted

do {
    let encodePerson = try jsonEncoder.
encode(person)
    let endcodeStringPerson = String(data:
encodePerson, encoding: .utf8)!
    print(endcodeStringPerson)
} catch {
    print(error.localizedDescription)
}
```

Date Formats

- **iso8601:** This will be a String type in the JSON object. A date formatted as: 1990–12–15T00:00:00Z. To convert this value to a Swift Date object, set the dateDecodingStrategy to .iso8601:

```
let person = """
{
    "name": "John",
    "age": 20,
    "birthDate":
"1990-12-15T00:00:00Z",
}
"""
let jsonDecoder = JSONDecoder()
jsonDecoder.dateDecodingStrategy =
.iso8601//1990-12-15T00:00:00Z
```

- **secondsSince1970:** This will be a Int type in the JSON object. A date formatted as: 661219200. To convert this value to a Swift Date object, set the dateDecodingStrategy to .secondsSince1970:

```
let person2 = """
{
    "name": "John",
    "age": 20,
    "birthDate": 661219200,
}
"""
let jsonDecoder2 = JSONDecoder()
jsonDecoder2.dateDecodingStrategy =
.secondsSince1970//661219200
```

- **Custom:** A date can be formatted as a string in several different ways. This is where the custom option is required. You can create an instance of the DateFormatter class and set the dateFormat with the custom string representing the data format:

```
let person3 = """
{
    "name": "John",
    "age": 20,
    "birthDate": "1990/12/15",
}
"""
let jsonDecoder3 = JSONDecoder()
let dateFomatter = DateFormatter()
dateFomatter.dateFormat = "yyyy/MM/dd"
jsonDecoder3.dateDecodingStrategy =
.formatted(dateFomatter)
```

As you can see, working with JSON is pretty easy in Swift. Nested JSON can get complicated quickly, but at least you have more than one option in this case.

WORKING WITH XML

A multitude of document formats using XML syntax had been developed, therefore it is essential to know how to work with them. In case you are not familiar with XML, it could be described as a precisely formatted text or string, which can be parsed into an array of objects containing the precious information. The key tool applied is the XMLParser, an event-driven parser of XML documents.

An XMLParser is mainly used to notify about the items (elements, attributes, and comments) that it encounters as it processes an XML document. It does not itself do anything with those parsed items except report them. For convenience, an XMLParser object in the following section is sometimes referred to as a parser object. Unless used in a callback, the XMLParser is a thread-safe class as long as any given instance is only used in one thread. The list of XMLParser basic features includes the following items:[7]

- **Initializing a Parser Object**

  - **init?(contentsOf: URL):** Initializes a parser with the XML content referenced by the given URL

  - **init(data: Data):** Initializes a parser with the XML contents encapsulated in a given data object

  - **init(stream: InputStream):** Initializes a parser with the XML contents from the specified stream and parses it

- **Managing Delegates**

  - **var delegate: XMLParserDelegate?:** A delegate object that receives messages about the parsing process

- **Managing Parser Behavior**

  - **var shouldProcessNamespaces: Bool:** A Boolean value that determines whether the parser reports the namespaces and qualified names of elements

---

[7] https://developer.apple.com/documentation/foundation/xmlparser, Apple

- **var shouldReportNamespacePrefixes: Bool:** A Boolean value that determines whether the parser reports the prefixes indicating the scope of namespace declarations

- **var shouldResolveExternalEntities: Bool:** A Boolean value that determines whether the parser reports declarations of external entities

- **Parsing**

  - **func parse() -> Bool:** Starts the event-driven parsing operation

  - **func abortParsing():** Stops the parser object

  - **var parserError: Error?:** An NSError object from which you can obtain information about a parsing error

- **Obtaining Parser State**

  - **var columnNumber: Int:** The column number of the XML document being processed by the parser

  - **var lineNumber: Int:** The line number of the XML document being processed by the parser

  - **var publicID: String?:** The public identifier of the external entity referenced in the XML document

  - **var systemID: String?:** The system identifier of the external entity referenced in the XML document

- **Constants**

  - **enum XMLParser.ExternalEntityResolvingPolicy:**
    class let errorDomain: String

  - Indicates an error in XML parsing

  - **enum XMLParser.ErrorCode:** The following
    error codes are defined by NSXMLParser. For
    error codes not listed here, see the <libxml/xml-
    error.h> header file

Let us start with the XMLParser. First of all, you need to
create the following custom objects:

```
class Item {
    var author = "";
    var desc = "";
    var tag = [Tag]();
}
class Tag {
    var name = "";
    var count: Int?;
}
```

Here, we created a separate class for every member, which
can get multiple values within its parent. Now, in order to
make this XML file digestible for Xcode, you need to create
a parser and set its delegate:

```
let xmlData = xmlString.dataUsingEncoding(
NSUTF8StringEncoding)!
let parser = NSXMLParser(data: xmlData)
parser.delegate = self;
parser.parse()
```

The delegate contains many functions, but these are the four main ones:

1. **func parser(didStartElement):** is called every time the parser finds a <key>

2. **func parser(didEndElement):** is called every time the parser finds a <key>

3. **func parser(foundCharacters):** is called every time the parser enters a and it will stop on line breaks and "special characters" (e.g., í, ö)

4. **func parserDidEndDocument:** is called when the parser finished the document

Now, that you know how our parser operates, we need to parse the elements. For this you will need a new Item array, an empty string for the found characters, and a global item variable similar to this one:

```
var items = [Item]();
var item = Item();
var foundCharacters = "";
```

After that you can apply the following delegate's methods:

```
func parser(parser: NSXMLParser,
didStartElement elementName: String,
namespaceURI: String?, qualifiedName qName:
String?, attributes attributeDict: [String
: String]) {
        if elementName == "tag" {
             let tempTag = Tag();
```

```
            if let name =
attributeDict["name"] {
                tempTag.name = name;
            }
            if let c =
attributeDict["count"] {
                if let count = Int(c) {
                    tempTag.count =
count;
                }
            }
            self.item.tag.append(tempTag);
    }
}
```

One thing to mention here is that if you have an in-line value (), you will not be able to use the didEndElement, since there is no value. Luckily, the attributeDict [String: String] dictionary is quite helpful with that. You just need to regulate which value you want to get and set. Another feature to note is the foundCharacters variable. The previously introduced parser(foundCharacters) function can be interrupted, but the parser parses the whole document synchronously, so it continues from where it stopped. To illustrate with an example:

```
func parser(parser: NSXMLParser,
didEndElement elementName: String,
namespaceURI: String?, qualifiedName qName:
String?) {
    if elementName == "author" {
        self.item.author = self.
foundCharacters;
    }
```

```
if elementName == "description" {
        self.item.desc = self.
foundCharacters;
    }

    if elementName == "item" {
        let tempItem = Item();
        tempItem.author = self.item.
author;
        tempItem.desc = self.item.desc;
        tempItem.tag = self.item.tag;
        self.items.append(tempItem);
        self.item.tag.removeAll();
    }
    self.foundCharacters = ""
}
```

You should notice, that you empty the foundCharacters value when the parser reaches the end of an element. Therefore, the fragments will give us the final string we wanted:

```
func parserDidEndDocument(parser:
XMLParser) {
    for item in self.items {
        print("\(item.author)\n\(item.
desc)");
        for tags in item.tag {
            if let count = tags.
count {
                print("\(tags.
name), \(count)")
            } else {
```

```
                        print("\(tags.
name)")
                }
            }
            print("\n")
        }
}
```

The only downside of the XMLParser is that you will have to work with 3-4 delegate functions, but they will be relatively short. Plus, you can use native protocol.

To summarize this chapter, we described the most popular methods for fetching Data with URLSession. We also defined the essential and the optional instruments when working with JSON and XML. The next chapter will complete the Swift toolset by learning about the core components of Xcode. We shall also review some of the most useful shortcuts and button techniques that one might need when building an iOS App with Cocoa Touch and integrating XCTest.

CHAPTER 5

Creating iOS Apps with Swift

IN THIS CHAPTER

➢ Reviewing core components of Xcode

➢ Building an iOS App with Cocoa Touch

➢ Unit and Integration Testing with XCTest

In the previous chapter, we learned Swift Standard Library, reviewed how to complete projects with JSON and XML. This chapter will go through creating iOS Apps with Swift and interacting with Xcode's main components and widgets.

Xcode is a great integrated development environment (IDE) produced by Apple for developing software for macOS, iOS, watchOS, and tvOS. It is the only officially supported tool for creating and publishing apps to Apple's

DOI: 10.1201/9781003254089-5

app store and is created for use by experienced developers as well as beginners. Xcode could also be viewed as a code editor, and it supports a huge variety of programming languages—C, C++, Objective-C, Objective-C++, Java, AppleScript, Python, Ruby, ResEdit, and Swift. In addition, it uses Cocoa, Carbon, and Java programming models.

Xcode has all of the tools needed to create an app within one software package; namely, a text editor, a compiler, and a build system. With Xcode, you can script, compile, and debug your app, and once you are finished, you can submit it to the Apple app store. It consists of a number of tools to help the development process move quickly so that developers can create apps lightning fast, and beginners face less uncertainty and barriers to starting a great application.

Basically, the tool is designed to give you one window in which to operate as a developer. It has a source code checker and autocomplete feature, which will make writing source code much easier. When you create a new project, you can choose from the available templates and stored snippets of code to give you a basic foundation on which to build. You can create your own templates if you find you are often retyping commonly-used code. These features allow beginners to use these templates to create their app even with little knowledge of application development. Advanced developers will also find these features help to streamline their assignment and make the application development process much smoother.

Moreover, Xcode comes with great debugging tools that allow developers to fix problems in their apps faster. It also has a variety of project management tools that allow you to manage your image assets and code files in an organized manner. It even has a source code checker that will highlight any errors while you are scripting, and then give solutions on how to correct the errors.

You can view all of your files at one time in the Xcode editor. Meaning that rather than having to open multiple files to make a small change, you can view them all and use the find and replace tool to update lines of your code. This will save your time in development and automatically save your work, so there is no need to worry about losing any updates or changes you have introduced.

Although there are other third-party IDEs that will let you create an iOS app outside of MacOS, they are more likely to fall short with testing and debugging. To make a truly multifunctional app, you will have to run it through testing and debugging. Thus, you want to test your app for core functionality to make sure that your app's main function or functions are administering as they should be and as experts will expect them to work. You also want to test the user interface (UI) to ensure that everything flows and works as it should from a user perspective. And every time you discover and fix a bug, it is recommended to write and run an additional test for your bug fix.

As mentioned, Xcode is the only supported way to develop apps by Apple. So in case you are interested in building iOS or macOS apps you have to use it. There are third-party solutions that do not require you to use Xcode, however, these are not supported by Apple and therefore often have issues with these solutions.

And since Xcode was created by Apple to help developers create iOS apps, the whole procedure of getting your app into the Apple app store is quite straightforward. Xcode makes it very easy to make your app available, you are only expected to upload your app to App Store Connect, test it, and then submit it for review and approval. Additionally, App Store Connect will allow you to monitor sales, view reports, and respond to reviews. In your App Store Connect account, you can enable TestFlight beta testing feature that will send beta builds of your app to testers for feedback. To put it simply, every application has to be approved by the Apple team for technical, design, and content guidelines before it will be available in the app store. The overall approval process can take 2–3 weeks.

CORE COMPONENTS OF XCODE

The Xcode IDE is at the core of the Apple development experience. It is an incredibly productive environment that has a great potential to take you from ideas, to script, to customers. Xcode even communicates with the Apple developer website, so you can enable services such as Game Center or Passbook in your app with a single click. When your app is ready, Xcode will set and submit your app to the App Store.

Because everything is so well integrated, the overall workflow feels almost effortless. For instance, as you combine a new interface, the Assistant editor intuitively displays the related source code in a split window pane. Apple LLVM compiler technologies offer to parse your code, keeping every symbol you see in the LLDB debugger consistent with the editor and compiler. That same engine is constantly operating as you type, finding mistakes and presenting Fix-its for your code. Let us review essential tools of Xcode in detail here:

- **Assistant Editor:** The Assistant button divides the Xcode editor in two, with your primary work document on the left and an intelligent Assistant editor pane to the right. The editor automatically displays files that Xcode marks are most helpful to you based on your primary editor's work. For instance, if you are editing MyProject.m in the primary editor, the Assistant will automatically show the counterpart MyProject.h. Moreover, you can work on the graphical design side-by-side with the implementation source code with the Assistant editor. Thus, a simple mouse drag from a UI control to the source pane creates a connection between code and interface, and can even create the code stub for you.

  Clicking the Jump Bar, placed at the top of every editor pane, you can quickly choose what information to view in the Assistant editor. For example, while editing source code in the primary editor, the Assistant can display the counterpart header, subclasses or superclasses, or related tests. Therefore, the Jump Bar could be viewed as a path control at the top of every editor pane that can be clicked to quickly jump to a new location or begin typing to filter down to a specific file or method definition.

- **Interface Builder:** Fully integrated within the Xcode IDE, the Interface Builder design canvas makes it incredibly easy to prototype a full UI without scripting any code. You can prototype in minutes, then graphically connect your interface to the source within the Xcode editor, laying out windows, buttons, and sliders to create a functioning Mac, iPhone, or iPad UI.

- **Version Editor and Source Control:** The Version editor allows you to compare two versions of a file, see commit logs, check who made a code change and even zoom back through the commit timeline. It helps you identify blame and graphically goes back in time to compare source files, with full support for Subversion and Git source control (SCM) systems. The Version editor divides the pane to show two different versions of the same file. The main differences would be highlighted as you go through the timeline separating the editor's views.

- **Testing:** Test-driven development is a first-class workflow within Xcode. The built-in Test Navigator allows you to jump to any test in your project, run an individual test, or complete a group of tests. The Assistant editor has new test-specific views that automatically track which tests exercise the code you are presently editing, keeping your tests and code in sync at all times.

- **Customize:** The Xcode environment can be configured to support almost any workflow, including customization features like tabs, behaviors, and snippets:

    - **Tabs:** You can create a completely unique layout of your project with tabs. Each tab has its own navigator, editor, assistant, and utility area arrangement.

It is possible to name tabs for specific tasks, rearrange them, or even remove the tab to create a stand-alone window.

- **Behaviors:** You can tell Xcode what to do with events such as starting a debug session or encountering an error during a build. Coupled with tabs, you can program a custom work environment for each of your edit, design, build, or debug projects. Custom behaviors can also completely re-arrange your window with a single key combination.

- **Snippets:** A variety of pre-configured code completions, such as defining a new class or method, are included in the snippets library. By customizing or adding snippets, you can add frequently entered code by scripting only a few characters.

- **Open Quickly:** Basically, you can get quick access to any file of your project using the Open Quickly Command-Shift-O. Xcode immediately offers completions for your search, allowing you to choose one and hit Return to open the file or hit Option-Return to open in the Assistant editor. In addition, shortened Application Programming Interface (API) documentation is displayed while you are programming, including comments that you add to your code.

- **Schemes:** It is acceptable to customize the way Xcode builds and runs your app depending on whether you are debugging, profiling, performing code analysis, or running a test suite. For instance, the default scheme is set to build your app in "Debug" mode when running, and the same scheme settings will build for "Release" when performing the Profile or Archive command. There is no need to edit project settings as you move from task to task as Xcode configures the schemes for you automatically.

- **Source Editor:** With Source Editor, you can write your code with advanced code completion, code folding, syntax highlighting, and message bubbles that display a warning, errors, and other context-sensitive information.

- **Compilers:** The powerful open-source compiler for C, C++, and Objective-C is built into Xcode and available from Terminal. With it, your code compiles quickly and is optimized by Apple to produce multifunctional apps specifically modified for the CPUs in iPhone, iPad, and Mac.

- **Continuous Integration:** Xcode Server regulates server-side bots that continuously build, analyze, test, and even archive your Xcode projects. The Xcode IDE can configure these bots, analyze nightly build and test results, and can track down which check-in broke the build.

- **Asset Catalog:** The asset catalog editor in Xcode manages your app's images, combining together various resolutions of the same asset. When building, Xcode sets the asset catalog into the most efficient bundle for final distribution.

- **OpenGL Frame Capture:** You can capture a complete representation of the current OpenGL frame from an iOS device by pressing a single button. Xcode displays the shader information, and can visually construct how the frame was designed within the Xcode debugger.

- **Live Issues:** Similar to a word processor that highlights spelling errors, Live Issues highlights common coding mistakes, without the need to click "build" first.

- **Fix-it:** Yet Xcode goes beyond just reporting errors. Thus, when you make a coding mistake, Xcode will immediately alert you, and a single keyboard shortcut will instantly fix the issue, so you will not miss a beat while coding.

- **XCTest Framework:** XCTest APIs make it easy to build unit tests that stretch app functionality and are capable of running on Mac, iPad, iPhone, or Simulator.

- **Static Analysis:** With Static Analyzer, you can find bugs in your code before the app is even run by letting it try out thousands of possible code paths in a few seconds. As a result, you will get a report of potential bugs that could have otherwise remained hidden.

There are also a few important Xcode development tools that you can launch independently from the Xcode > Open Developer Tool menu:

- **Use Simulator** for rapid prototyping and testing your app in a simulated environment when a real device is not available. The simulator provides environments for iPhone, iPad, Apple Watch, and Apple TV devices with different settings, files, and operating system options. The simulator has great features such as:

- Prototyping and debugging your apps

- Optimizing your graphics

- Interacting with your apps on iOS, watchOS, and tvOS using your pointer and keyboard

- Testing your apps

Installed as part of the Xcode tools, Simulator runs on your Mac and could be viewed as a standard Mac app while simulating iPhone, iPad, Apple Watch, or Apple TV environments. Each simulated device and software version combination is considered its own simulation environment, separate from others, with its own configurations and files. These settings and files exist on every device you test within a simulation environment. You can open multiple simulated devices for interactions such as an iPhone and a paired Apple watch.

- **Use Instruments** to set and analyze your app, advance performance, and find memory problems. Fundamentally, instruments is a powerful and flexible performance-analysis and testing tool that is part of the Xcode toolset. It is incorporated to help you profile your iOS, watchOS, tvOS, and macOS apps, processes, and devices in order to better and optimize their behavior and operability. Including Instruments into your work base from the beginning of the app development process can save you time later by helping you detect issues early in the development project.

However, unlike other performance and debugging tools, Instruments allows you to gather widely disparate types of data and examine them side by side. This makes it easier to spot trends that might otherwise be overlooked. For instance, your app may have a large memory growth caused by multiple open network connections. By using the Allocations and Connections instruments at the same time, you can identify connections that are not closing and thus resulting in rapid memory growth. By applying Instruments effectively, you can:

- perform profiling in a simulator or on a physical device;

- find out problems in your source code;

- see memory problems in your apps, such as leaks, abandoned memory, and zombies;

- find ways to optimize your app for greater power efficiency;

- assess the behavior of one or more apps or processes;

- examine device-specific features, such as Wi-Fi and Bluetooth;

- complete performance analysis on your app;

- run general system-level troubleshooting; and

- save instrument configurations as templates.

- **Use Create ML** to create and try custom machine learning models for your app. It is possible to train models to recognize images, extract meaning from text, or find relationships between numerical values. You can also train a model to recognize patterns by showing representative samples. For instance, you can train a model to recognize dogs by showing it lots of images of different dogs. After you have trained the model, you test it out on data it has not seen before, and evaluate how well it completed the task. When the model is performing well enough, you can integrate it into your app using Core ML.

- **Use Reality Composer** to construct 3D compositions and augmented reality (AR) experiences. Apple's Reality Composer app can offer you an intuitive interface for constructing 3D compositions and AR experiences. You combine 3D models, audio, and other items—along with a description of how these objects behave—into a file that you include in your RealityKit-enabled app. You can also export your composition as a lightweight AR Quick Look experience that lets users place and preview content.

You typically start by choosing the kind of real-world object that should anchor your scene, like a horizontal surface or the user's face. Then position virtual elements within your scene by selecting from Reality Composer's large collection of customizable assets, or import your own in usdz format. Then you can add animations and sound-triggered by events like user taps, as well as behaviors driven by the physics simulation.

If you are composing on a Mac, you can synchronize your composition with Reality Composer on an iOS device to try it in an AR session. Alternatively, try composing directly on the iOS device. Either way, you would be expected to use the RealityKit framework in your app to load, simulate, and render the composition. Anyway, you automatically get Reality Composer for macOS when you install Xcode 11 or later since the app is one of the developer tools bundled with Xcode.

The first time you open the app, or when you start a new project with the File > New menu option, Reality Composer prompts you to choose an anchor. An anchor stands for the real-world reference around which you build your composition. When a user later works with a scene in an AR app, ARKit looks for a real-world item that matches your anchor and attaches your scene to that.

Linking content to a particular point in space creates the perception that your content is part of the real world. By selecting an appropriate anchor, you ensure that users decode your content in a sensible way. For instance, to create a scene that is supposed to exist on a tabletop, like a collection of wooden blocks, choose a horizontal plane. That way, the components that you add to the scene appear to rest on the table.

Creating an Xcode Project for an App

Now let us look at how you can start developing your app by creating an Xcode project from a template. In order to create an Xcode project for your app, you should choose a template for the platform on which your app will run, and select the type of app you need to develop, such as a single view, game, or document-based for iOS. Keep in mind that Xcode templates include essential project configuration and files that help you start developing your app quickly.

Before you create a project, you would be expected to collect the information that Xcode needs to identify your app and register you as a developer:[1]

- **Product name.** The name of your app will be displayed in the App Store and appear on a device when installed. The product name must be at least 2 characters and no more than 255 bytes and should be similar to the app name that you enter later in App Store Connect.

- **Organization identifier.** A reverse DNS string that uniquely identifies your organization. If you do not have a company identifier, use com.example followed by your organization name, and replace it before you distribute your app.

- **Organization name.** The name appears in boilerplate text throughout your project folder. For instance, the source and header file copyright strings contain the organization name. The organization name in your project is not the same as the organization name that appears in the App Store.

Another notable thing is, the organization identifier should be counted as part of the ID bundle (CFBundleIdentifier) by default. Xcode uses the bundle ID to register an App ID when you first run your app on a device. The number

---

[1] https://developer.apple.com/documentation/xcode/creating-an-xcode-project-for-an-app, Apple

of App IDs is limited if you are not a member of the Apple
Developer Program. You are not permitted to change the
App ID after you upload a build to App Store Connect
Therefore, make sure to choose the organization identifier
carefully.

You can create a Project by launching Xcode, then clicking "Create a new Xcode project" in the Welcome to Xcode
window or choose File > New > Project. In the screen that
appears, select the target operating system or platform and
a template under Application. In the following sheets, you
should fill out the forms and choose options to configure
your project. You must provide a product name and organization identifier because they are used to create the bundle
identifier that identifies your app throughout the system.
In order to develop for all platforms and see an interactive
preview of your layout, choose SwiftUI as the UI before you
click Next on this sheet.

Managing Files in the Main Window
When you create a project or open an existing project, the
main window appears, showing the necessary files and
resources for developing your app. You can access different
sections of your project from the navigator area in the main
window. Use the same project navigator to select files you
want to edit in the editor area. For instance, when you choose
a Swift file in the project navigator, the file opens in the source
editor, where you can edit the code and set breakpoints.

Detailed information about the selected file also appears
in the inspector area on the right. In the inspector area, you
can select the Attributes inspector to modify the properties
of a file or UI component. If you need to hide the inspector

to make more space for the editor, simply click the "Hide or show the Inspectors" button in the upper-right corner of the toolbar.

You use the same toolbar to build and run your app on a simulated or real device. For iOS apps, choose the app target and a simulator or device from the run destination menu in the toolbar, then click the Run button. For macOS apps, just click the Run button. When your app launches, the debug area opens, where you can control the execution of your app and inspect variables. When the app stops at the breakpoint, just activate the controls in the debug area to step through the code or continue execution. When you are done running the app, do not forget to click the Stop button in the toolbar.

In case you are using SwiftUI, you can see an interactive preview of the UI while you are creating your app. Xcode keeps track of all the changes you introduce to the source file, the canvas on the right, and the inspector in sync. You can use the controls in the preview to regulate the app with the debugger as well.

In order to change properties you entered when creating your project, select the project name in the project navigator that appears at the top, then the project editor opens in the editor area. Most of the properties you entered should appear on the General pane of the project editor.

BUILDING AN IOS APP WITH COCOA TOUCH

Cocoa is a collection of tools—libraries, frameworks, and APIs—applied to build applications for the Mac OS. Most of the basic functionality you would need to develop a rich Mac application is included in Cocoa. There are mechanisms for drawing to display, working with text, saving and opening data files, regulating the operating system, and even connecting to other computers across a network. Basically, the look and feel of Mac applications that are recognizable and appreciated by many in large part are due to the breadth and quality of the Cocoa UI framework.

The Cocoa framework has two fundamental areas of focus: classes that represent UI objects and collect user input, and classes that tackle challenges like memory management, networking, file system operations, and time management.

Creating applications for the iPhone and iPod Touch is similar in many ways to building applications for Mac OS X. The same tools are included for writing and debugging code, laying out visual interfaces, and profiling performance, but mobile application development requires a supplemental set of software libraries and tools, called the iPhone software development kit (SDK).

Cocoa Touch stands for a modified version of Cocoa with device-specific libraries for the iPhone and iPod Touch. Cocoa Touch operates in great collaboration with other layers in the iPhone and iPod Touch operating systems and is the key focus of this section.

Normally, Mac OS X programmers use a framework called AppKit that supplies all the windows, buttons, menus, graphics contexts, and event handling methods that have come to define the OS X experience. The Cocoa Touch equivalent is called UIKit. In addition to UI elements, UIKit has event handling mechanisms and allows drawing to the screen. UIKit is a very multifaceted framework and is a major focus of user experience programmers. Nearly all UI needs are accounted for in UIKit, and developers can produce custom UI elements very easily.

The second Cocoa Touch framework is the Foundation framework. One should perceive Foundation as the layer that abstracts many of the underlying operating system elements such as primitive types, bundle management, file operations, and networking from the UI objects in UIKit. To put it simply, Foundation is the gateway to everything that is not a part of the UI. And it is important to understand that user experience programming goes deeper than the UI, it regulates and includes things such as latency management, error handling, data caching, and data persistence.

UIKit Overview

The UI consists of the elements of an application that users see, click, and—in the case of Cocoa Touch—tilt, shake, or tap. UIs are a huge part of the user experience as they provide the face of your product.

For the most part, UIKit could be viewed as just a limited subset of the AppKit framework for Mac OS X. And in case you have experience developing Cocoa apps for the Mac, you will get your head around UIKit very quickly. The main differences are that UIKit is tuned for specific hardware interfaces and that it provides less functionality than AppKit. The reduced scope of UIKit is primarily due to the differences in inoperability between typical computers and the iPhone or iPod Touch. Despite the omission of a few familiar elements, UIKit is a very reliable toolset.

The core class from which all Cocoa objects inherit basic behavior is NSObject. The NS prefix has roots in the non-Apple origins of Cocoa at NeXT. The early versions of what is now Cocoa were called NextStep. Most Cocoa classes in Cocoa are subclasses of NSObject, and many classes assume that NSObject is the foundation of objects being passed around. For instance, the class NSArray, which represents a collection of pointers, requires that any pointer it stores points to an NSObject subclass. In most cases, any custom class you create should inherit from NSObject.

In addition, all UIKi classes that respond to user input inherit from UIResponder, which is an NSObject subclass that provides functionality around handling user input. In addition to the UIResponder class hierarchy, UIKit includes a set of classes acting as value objects, logical controllers, and hardware features.

The Foundation Overview

The Foundation layer of Cocoa Touch provides an object-oriented abstraction to the core components of the operating system. Foundation has the capacity to manage core features of Cocoa Touch, including:[2]

- Essential object behavior, such as memory management mechanisms

- Inter-object notification mechanisms, such as event dispatching

- Access to resource bundles (files bundled with your application)

- Internationalization and localization of resources, such as text strings and images

- Data management tools (SQLite, filesystem access)

- Object wrappers of primitive types, such as NSInteger, NSFloat, and NSString

---

[2] https://www.oreilly.com/library/view/programming-the-iphone/9780596805760/ch01.html, O'Reilly

All Cocoa Touch applications must be connected against Foundation because Foundation contains the classes that make a Cocoa application work—including many classes that are essential in the functioning of the UI framework. For instance, many UIKit methods use NSString objects as arguments or return values from methods.

One significant difference between the iPhone OS and Mac OS X is that the implementation of Foundation for Cocoa Touch does not automatically recover memory when objects get damaged. This means developers should keep track of the objects they create and be careful when following certain idioms in order to keep memory usage as low as possible.

Typically, when you write an iOS application, you just import the Foundation or UIKit framework and think nothing of it. You might 'import Foundation' if you want to work with Strings, Dates, the file system, or threads, while you might import UIKit if you want to use UITableViewController or UIAlertController. If you're importing UIKit then you can forget Foundation altogether, since UIKit does it behind the scenes anyway.

Each of these frameworks is built by Apple. They are available to developers so everyone can take advantage of the technologies that make iOS apps successful. The best reason to use frameworks is that they can be built once and be reused an infinite number of times. For example, UIKit is developed by Apple and is constantly being updated. It is a project that developers can repeatedly reuse to build new applications or define awesome functionality in projects like animation, (UI)Buttons, transitions, and (UI)Colors.

Creating Frameworks

We can now attempt to build a framework to mimic the custom status alerts that Apple has been using across iOS. These alerts are relatively simple and only consist of a UIVisualEffectView as the background, an UIImage, and some text.

Get started by opening Xcode and creating a new project. Select the iOS tab, scroll down to Framework & Library and select Cocoa Touch Framework. You can name the new project ModalStatusView. Then create another file, but this time under UI select View and name it ModalStatusView. xib. A XIB file shall further be used as a storyboard, except that it is meant for a single view instead of a set of them.

After that, open the XIB file and delete the view that is currently there. Now just like with a storyboard, you can add some objects to the view that will comprise the custom 'ModalStatusView'. To do that, simply drag an Image View and two Labels to the visual effects view. And since a XIB is a single view in a file, you should assign classes to the 'File's Owner' section.

With that, you are ready to start mixing the XIB with code. It is better to start by making some outlets for the most important objects in the view, the image, and the two labels. Select the Assistant Editor so that you can view the .xib and .swift files simultaneously and then add a basic class like so:

```
class ModalStatusView: UIView {
}
```

Just as you would in a storyboard, control+click and drag each element inside of the class that we created a few minutes ago. If you have trouble adding the outlets, build a new project and try again. If that does not work make sure that you set the File Owner's class to "ModalStatusView" and not the view's class.

Now you can go back to the standard editor and forget about the XIB file for a bit. Open ModalStatusView.swift. And since we will be creating public functions to edit these properties, it is recommended to hide access to the raw outlets by adding the following code after the outlets:[3]

```
// MARK: Set Up View
public override init(frame: CGRect) {
// For use in code
  super.init(frame: frame)
  setUpView()
}

public required init?(coder aDecoder:
NSCoder) {
    // For use in Interface Builder
    super.init(coder: aDecoder)
    setUpView()
}
```

These two initializers (public override init and public required init?) are what Xcode starts with when it will create a new ModalStatusView. The first one can be run directly from code, while the second is needed to work in Interface Builder.

You may have noticed that the setUpView() function has not been created yet. Mainly because before we add func

---

[3] https://medium.com/flawless-app-stories/getting-started-with-reusable-frameworks-for-ios-development-f00d74827d11, Medium

setUpView(), we need to add some supporting variables. Add the following to the class just below the outlets:

```
let nibName = "ModalStatusView"
var contentView: UIView!
```

Now we are ready to add setUpView() to the file. Add the following code after the last initializer that we scripted:[4]

```
private func setUpView() {
    let bundle = Bundle(for: type(of:
self))
    let nib = UINib(nibName: self.nibName,
bundle: bundle)
    self.contentView = nib.
instantiate(withOwner: self, options: nil).
first as! UIView
    addSubview(contentView)

    contentView.center = self.center
    contentView.autoresizingMask = []
    contentView.
translatesAutoresizingMaskIntoConstraints
= true

    headlineLabel.text = ""
    subheadLabel.text = ""
}
```

There's a good amount going on here, but first, we need to set the variable contentView to be the view inside out our XIB

---

[4] https://medium.com/flawless-app-stories/getting-started-with-reusable-frameworks-for-ios-development-f00d74827d11, Medium

file that we created. This is done by accessing the Bundle for this framework, the NIB (which references a compiled XIB), and finally the view inside of the NIB. Following that, we want to add the contentView that we just created to this class's view by using addSubview(contentView).

We'll then set the frame of the contentView equal to the bounds of the parent view in the class. After that, we want to tell it that we don't approve of any resizing since this view has a specific size. That is why we passed the autoresizingMask an empty array. Finally, we want to set the labels to have empty text inside, so that our framework is completely customizable.

One last thing before you can build and use the framework is to mark the outlets as being private by adding these three functions so that the framework's potential users can set the image and label outlets from their code:

```
// Provide functions to update view
public func set(image: UIImage) {
    self.statusImage.image = image
}
 public func set(headline text: String) {
    self.headlineLabel.text = text
}
public func set(subheading text: String) {
    self.subheadLabel.text = text
}
```

With that, we have a framework ready, yet since it does not do much by itself, let us test it out.

We shall create a new project to test out the framework. Start by going to your Project Inspector's General tab and add another embedded binary. A Finder window will drop down, and here you need to select the ModalStatus. xcodeproj framework that you created earlier. You should be able to notice that the Framework was added to the Project Navigator.

Now go back to Embedded Binaries and check the new framework that we added earlier. Give the project a quick build (command+B) to make sure that things are going well so far. At this point, there should not be any errors yet.

Now that you have our own framework, we need to make sure that Xcode is actually referencing it before you can start coding towards it. Jump to the ViewController. swift file and import ModalStatus just below import UIKit. ViewController.swift has an action that is performed when the user hits "Save" while viewing a picture. Add present-ModalStatusView() inside of the saveTapped(_:) function. And after that add the presentModalStatusView() function to the class so that the compiler will leave this code alone:

```
func presentModalStatusView() {
    let modalView = ModalStatusView(frame:
self.view.bounds)
    let downloadImage = UIImage(named:
"download") ?? UIImage()
    modalView.set(image: downloadImage)
    modalView.set(headline: "Downloading")
    view.addSubview(modalView)
}
```

A few things happened here. First, we initialized an ModalStatusView and named it modalView. Then we created an UIImage using the "download.png" image stored in the assets. Then we set the image and some text to the view and added it to the ViewController as a subview. You can try to build and run the application on the simulator now. It should work yet lack efficiency in the following areas:

Timer

In order to set the timer, tap the drop down next to the framework's project and navigate to the ModalStatusView. swift file that we created a while ago. The first step is to enable the view to close itself after a given few seconds. Add var timer: Timer? after the declaration of the contentView variable. Then add the following code:

```
public override func didMoveToSuperview()
{
    // Add a timer to remove the view
        self.timer = Timer.scheduledTimer(
            timeInterval: TimeInterval(3.0),
            target: self,
            selector: #selector(self.
removeSelf),
            userInfo: nil,
            repeats: false)
}
@objc private func removeSelf() {
    self.removeFromSuperview()
}
```

Basically, this is a simple code to tell the project: "Remove this view after three seconds have passed."

Rounded Corners

Next is rounded corners, which seriously reduce the sharpness of the ModalStatusView. Add the following code to the class as well:

```
// Allow view to control itself
public override func layoutSubviews() {
    // Rounded corners
    self.layoutIfNeeded()
    self.contentView.layer.masksToBounds =
true
    self.contentView.clipsToBounds = true
    self.contentView.layer.cornerRadius = 10
}
```

This is the typical code that can be applied to create rounded corners. The important parts to mention are that this is occurring after the subviews have been laid out and that we are setting clipsToBounds to true so that the subviews contained within contentView cannot slide out from behind the rounded corners.

Now there is only one thing left to do—let us add some animation.

Animation

The simplest and most effective way to add animations is to replace the didMoveToSuperview and removeSelf functions with the following:[5]

```
public override func didMoveToSuperview()
{
    // Fade in when added to superview
    // Then add a timer to remove the view
  self.contentView.transform =
CGAffineTransform(scaleX: 0.5, y: 0.5)
```

---

[5] https://medium.com/flawless-app-stories/getting-started-with-reusable-frameworks-for-ios-development-f00d74827d11, Medium

```
    UIView.animate(withDuration: 0.15,
animations: {
        self.contentView.alpha = 1.0
        self.contentView.transform =
CGAffineTransform.identity
    }) { _ in
        self.timer = Timer.scheduledTimer(
            timeInterval:
TimeInterval(3.0),
            target: self,
            selector: #selector(self.
removeSelf),
            userInfo: nil,
            repeats: false)
    }
}
@objc private func removeSelf() {
    // Animate removal of view
    UIView.animate(
        withDuration: 0.15,
        animations: {
        self.contentView.transform =
CGAffineTransform(scaleX: 0.5, y: 0.5)
        self.contentView.alpha = 0.0
    }) { _ in
        self.removeFromSuperview()
    }
}
```

And then add contentView.alpha = 0.0 to the end of
setUpView.

What is happening here isn't all that complicated. In
didMoveToSuperview we are transforming contentView
to half its width and height. Then we run animation with

UIView.animate(withDuration). We also set the alpha value back to 1.0 inside the animation. This tells content-View to grow from half its size as it fades in during the animation. After the animation finishes, we set the timer that was originally created. In removeSelf we are doing the opposite. During the animation, we want the alpha value to drop back to 0.0 (or transparent) and the transform to again make contentView half its usual size. After the animation is finished, we can get rid of the view altogether.

UNIT AND INTEGRATION TESTING XCTEST

Xcode has feature-rich software testing options for developers that can significantly help to advance the stability of the software. Moreover, Xcode provides XCTest and XCUITest that are extremely useful for achieving and building better quality software. Carefully tested apps, and regardless if done at unit level or UI level, improve the user experience and accelerate the adoption of those apps.

At the same time, XCTest is not a new framework and it has evolved quite well with Xcode releases. In fact, the XCTest framework was introduced with Xcode 5. What XCTest basically does is to permit its users to do unit testing for Xcode projects as it is currently considered as one of the top options for iOS app testing. And writing any tests with XCTest is a simple task to iOS developers because XCTest is fully compatible with both Objective-C and Swift.

In addition, XCTest tests can be implemented in simulators or real physical devices. If you use real devices locally, you just need to ensure all provisioning sides of things are accurate and set properly to test target. The test methods used in XCTest are instance methods, so no parameters are passed, nor do they return a value. For this, the name also begins with "test" and all added tests could be displayed in Test Navigator of your Xcode project.

Pros and Cons of XCTest Framework

Many modern test automation frameworks are based on frameworks and layers that development tools provide with them. In the case of iOS, this is XCTest and with Android, most of the frameworks are based on Android instrumentation. The advantages of XCTest over the other frameworks for iOS app testing include the following:

- **Easy to Learn with No Additional Components Required:** Xcode provides everything to get started with test automation with XCTest. Xcode's XCTest is an integral part of the tool, so testing is pretty easy to start and convenient to operate with.

- **Native iOS Language Support:** Typically writing tests with the same programming language that your application is built with is not a requirement, but it gives some reassurance for developers to create tests for their apps. Another way around, some developers may also think this differently and prefer other additional languages, frameworks, and tools to be used in test creation. Nevertheless, for iOS users, there is no learning curve or language barrier to get started with XCTest test creation.

- **Xcode Test Recorder:** This is mostly a characteristic for UI tests but as XCTest is closely related to XCUITest the UI recording is possible for Xcode environment as well. The UI testing capacities with Xcode include UI recording, generating code out of those recordings, and running tests identically as intended while the UI test was recorded. Record-and-playback testing tools have plenty of benefits and can get testers to complete the job even without understanding the underlying software. Additionally, recording tests again is possible or simply editing the generated piece of code with whatever changes have been done for the app itself. In short, record and playback tools provide a convenient way to create tests, an acceptable level of accuracy, and not being too sensitive for user-input errors.

- **Integrating with Continuous Integration:** Integrating XCTest with continuous integration is also pretty straightforward. Xcode allows XCTest tests to be implemented using command-line scripts/ shell and seamlessly integrated with Xcode's continuous integration Bots. However, there is a way to integrated XCTest scripts and the development environment with more widely used continuous integration systems, such as Jenkins, but there are too many things to keep track of sometimes—despite XCTest and Xcode have provided this capability for some time—tests end up failing just for no reason.

- **Faster Than "On-Top-of-It" Frameworks:** Many other frameworks are relying on XCTest. And despite that those frameworks having more features, higher abstraction levels for testing, and better capabilities, they still rely on the foundation of XCTest. This naturally makes XCTest faster as there is no need to rely on abstraction APIs, thus in many cases lightweight.

XCTest is not perfect in many ways, but it provides some excellent basic functionality and capabilities to exercise tests on your iOS apps. As XCTest has evolved with each version of Xcode, there are few cons you should be aware of:

- **No Cross-Platform Support:** Apple normally builds everything to be available only on their own tools, devices and environments. As this is understandable in the case of integral testing API and functionalities, many testers still prefer cross-platform test automation frameworks and have that one test script to work on both platforms, Android and iOS.

- **Limited Programming Language Support:** As this is one of iOS app development's advantages, it is also one of its cons. Basically, app developers and tests created for those apps are limited to build with Objective-C or Swift. Again, the preferred framework to many on top of XCTest would be the one that expands the programming language selection and provides testers freedom of choice with their tools and programming languages.

Additionally, XCTest still has some issues with the basic usability and the flexibility of creating tests for iOS apps. Doing some of the basic unit tests and running on those in simulators may work just fine, but when you try to run the same tests on devices, you might observe that there is some room for stability improvements with XCTest and Xcode in general.

In general, XCTest can facilitate your ability to write tests at different levels of abstraction. Its solid testing strategy combines multiple types of tests, to maximize the benefits of each, a large number of fast, well-isolated unit tests to cover your app's logic, and a smaller number of integration tests to demonstrate that smaller parts are connected together properly.

We shall also look at the UI tests as it could be considered as the ultimate indicator your app works for users in the way you expect, even if they take longer to run than other kinds of tests. These tests can demonstrate whether users can complete their tasks, and give you fast feedback about the correctness of your app's logic and the impact of changes you make. In addition to the UI test, you will also cover integration and performance tests to provide regression coverage of performance-critical components of code.

Writing a Unit Test

Each unit test should submit to the expected behavior of a single path through a method or function in your project. And in order to test multiple paths, you need to write one test for each scenario. For instance, if a function receives an optional parameter, you would have to write a test in which the parameter is nil and a test in which it takes a non-nil value. You can identify the boundary cases and logical branches in your code, and script a unit test to cover each combination of these cases.

Start by choosing the class or function to test, and create a subclass of XCTestCase that contains the tests for that class or function. Next, add a method to your XCTestCase subclass that takes no arguments and returns Void, giving the method a name that begins with the word "test." In Xcode, select New File, then select the Unit Test Case Class template to automatically create an appropriate class. The test method should contain the following three steps:

- **Arrange:** At this step, you should create any objects or data structures that the code path you are operating uses. Replace complex dependencies with "stubs" that are easy to configure to ensure that tests run quickly and efficiently. Adopting protocol-oriented programming ensures that connections between objects in your app are relatively flexible to enable the substitution of real implementations for stubs.

- **Act:** At this point, you are expected to call the method or function that you are testing, using parameters and properties that you modify in the Arrange phase.

- **Assert:** Access the Test Assertions in the XCTest framework to compare the behavior of the code you administer in the Act phase with your expectations of what should happen. Any assertion whose condition is false causes a test to fail. The resulting test method should look something like this:[6]

```
class MyAPITests: XCTestCase {
  func testMyAPIWorks() {
    // Arrange: create the necessary
dependencies.
    // Act: call my API, using the
dependencies created above.
```

---

[6] https://developer.apple.com/documentation/xcode/testing-your-apps-in-xcode, Apple

```
    XCTAssertTrue(/* … */, "The result
wasn't what I expected")
  }
}
```

Writing an Integration Test

Integration tests look very similar to unit tests—it applies the same APIs, and follows the same Arrange-Act-Assert pattern. The difference between a unit test and an integration test lies in the overall scale. While a unit test takes a very small part of your app's logic, an integration test covers the behavior of a larger subsystem or combination of classes and functions. Meaning that in the Arrange step of an integration test, you should widen the scope of the real project code under test, using fewer stub objects.

Therefore, rather than trying to review every different condition or boundary case as with unit tests, it could be beneficial to use integration tests to assert that components work together to achieve app goals in certain settings.

Writing a UI Test

You might want to run UI tests to verify that important user tasks can be completed in the app and that bugs that break the behavior of UI controls have not been introduced yet. UI tests are great as they replicate real user activities and provide confidence that the app can be utilized for its intended task. A UI test for a document-based app might also confirm that the user can start a new document, edit its content, then remove the document.

UI tests work in a different fashion from unit and integration tests, but they are still administered as methods on subclasses of XCTestCase. Xcode's UI Test Case Class template for new files consists of the basic starting points for UI tests. Thus, rather than implementing your app's code directly, they use the app's user-interface controls as a real user would, to examine whether the user would be able to complete a specific task via the app.

In order to create a UI test in a method on an XCTestCase subclass, you need to record your interaction with the app using Xcode's Record UI Test feature. Once you have recorded a workflow that exercises the functionality you are about to test, you can use the test assertion functions to ensure that the final state of the UI is what you would expect, given the actions performed during the recorded interaction.

Where UI tests emulate complex workflows comprising multiple distinct steps, use XCTActivity function in order to organize and name the shared steps. You can also create helper methods to share implementations of activities that are used in multiple tests.

Overall, designing UI tests to replicate the most critical workflows could cause the biggest impact to your users if they broke, and should be used to prevent any bugs and avoid potential regressions.

Writing a Performance Test

You would normally write performance tests to gain additional information on time taken, memory used, or data written, during the implementation of a region of code. XCTest goes through your code multiple times, reviewing the requested metrics. It is possible to set a baseline requirement for the metric, and if the measured value is significantly worse than the baseline, XCTest would immediately report a test failure.

In order to test the time taken by your code, call measure(_:) inside your test method, and run your app's code inside the block argument to measure(_:). And to examine maintenance using other metrics, including memory use and amount of data written to disk, call measure(metrics:block:) in the following manner:[7]

```
class PerformanceTests: XCTestCase {
  func testCodeIsFastEnough() {
    self.measure() {
      // performance-sensitive code here
    }
  }
}
```

To conclude this chapter, we have discussed the Xcode and its core components as well as learned how to build an iOS App with Cocoa Touch framework. In addition, we have established how you can manage Unit and Integration Testing with XCTest. In the next chapter, we shall cover the building blocks of SwiftUI, exploring Text and Decoration as well as creating Custom Views and Lists.

---

[7] https://developer.apple.com/documentation/xcode/testing-your-apps-in-xcode, Apple

CHAPTER 6

Building Blocks of SwiftUI

IN THIS CHAPTER

➤ Exploring building blocks of SwiftUI

➤ Creating Custom Views and Lists

➤ Learning about Declarative Syntax

In the previous chapter, we learned about the core Components of Xcode, reviewed its main advantages and disadvantages. This chapter shall cover building blocks of SwiftUI like Controls, Views, Lists, and Text. First, we shall look at the SwiftUI as a whole, explore Custom components, and then configure and declare the code's key components.

DOI: 10.1201/9781003254089-6

SwiftUI is a framework that provides views, controls, and layout structures for declaring your app's user interface (UI). It also makes use of event handlers for delivering taps, gestures, and other types of input to your app, as well as tools to administer the flow of data from your app's models down to the views and controls that users are going to interact with.

With this framework, you can define your app structure and populate it with scenes that contain the views that found your app's UI. Therefore, it is recommended to create your own custom views that conform to the View protocol and compose them with SwiftUI views for displaying text, images, and custom shapes using stacks, lists, and others. In addition, you can apply various modifiers to built-in views and your own views to customize their rendering and interactivity. After that, you can share code between apps on multiple platforms with views and controls that adapt to their context and assignment.

Moreover, you can integrate SwiftUI views with objects from the UIKit, AppKit, and WatchKit frameworks to take further advantage of platform-specific functionality. You can also customize accessibility support in SwiftUI, and localize your app's interface for different languages, countries, or cultural regions. This way SwiftUI helps you build great-looking apps across all Apple platforms bringing even better experiences to all users, on any Apple device, using just one set of tools and Application Programming Interfaces (APIs).

SwiftUI is very much committed to advancing app experiences and tools. It does so through enhancing your apps with new features, such as improved list views, better search experiences, and support for control focus areas.

At the same time, due to great accessibility improvements, SwiftUI has been able to speed up interactions by exposing the most relevant items on a screen in a simple list using the new Rotor API. The current accessibility focus state, such as the VoiceOver cursor, can now be read and even changed programmatically. And with the new Accessibility Representation API, your custom controls easily inherit full accessibility support from existing standard SwiftUI controls.

SWIFTUI IMPROVEMENTS ON MACOS

New SwiftUI performance and availability improvements, including support for multicolumn tables, make your macOS apps even better in the following essential areas.

Always-On Retina Display Support

On Apple Watch Series 5 and later, the Always-On Retina Display allows watchOS apps to stay visible, even when the watch face is dimmed, making key information available at a glance.

Widgets for iPadOS

With new SwiftUI improvements, now widgets can be placed anywhere on the Home screen and increased to a new, extra-large widget size.

Declarative Syntax

SwiftUI uses a declarative syntax, so you can simply regulate what your UI should do. For instance, you can script that you want a list of items consisting of text fields, then set alignment, font, and color for each field. Your code will be simpler and easier to read than ever before, saving you time and maintenance.

This declarative style also applies to complex concepts like animation. It is possible to easily add animation to almost any control and choose a collection of ready-to-use effects with only a few lines of code. The system manages all of the steps needed to maintain a smooth movement at runtime and even deals with interruption to keep your app stable.

DESIGN TOOLS

When it comes to Design Tools, Xcode includes intuitive design solutions that make building interfaces with SwiftUI as easy as dragging and dropping. Thus, as you work in the design canvas, everything you modify is completely in sync with the code in the adjoining editor. Code is instantly visible as a preview as you type, and any change you introduce to that preview immediately appears in your code. Xcode recompiles your changes instantly and inserts them into a running version of your app—visible, and flexible at all times. The main design tools available are the following:

- **Drag and drop:** You can organize components within your UI by simply dragging controls on the canvas. Just click to open an inspector to select font, color, alignment, and other design options, and easily rearrange controls with your cursor. Many of these visual editors are also accessible within the code editor, so you can use inspectors to discover new modifiers for each control, even if you would like to hand-code some bits of your interface. You can even drag controls from your library and drop them on the design canvas or directly on the code.

- **Dynamic replacement:** The Swift compiler and runtime are fully embedded throughout Xcode, meaning that your app is constantly being built and run even if you are not aware of it. The design canvas you see is not just an approximation of your UI — it is your whole live app. And Xcode can swap edited code directly in your live app with "dynamic replacement," which is a new feature in Swift.

- **Previews:** Creating one or many previews of any SwiftUI views is now possible to get sample data and modify almost anything your users might be presented with, such as large fonts, localization, or Dark Mode. Previews can also show your UI on any device or any orientation.

CONTROLS, VIEWS, AND LISTS

Views and controls should be perceived as the visual building blocks of your app's UI. You have to use them to present your app's content on screen. Views typically stand for text, images, shapes, custom drawings, and compositions of any and all of these together. And Controls enable user interaction with consistent APIs that adapt to their platform and context.

You can easily assemble the view's standard body by combining one or more of the primitive views provided by SwiftUI, like the Text instance plus other custom views that you want to define. At the same time, it is possible to create custom views simply by declaring types that conform to the View protocol. You can implement the required body computed property to provide the content for your custom view in the following manner:

```
struct MyView: View {
    var body: some View {
        Text("Hello, World!")
    }
}
```

The View protocol provides a set of modifiers or else known as protocol methods with default implementations that you apply to configure views in the layout of your app. Modifiers work by wrapping the view instance on which you call them in another view with the specified characteristics. For instance, adding the opacity(_:) modifier to a text view returns a new view with some amount of transparency:

```
Text("Hello, World!")
    .opacity(0.5) // Display partially
transparent text.
```

The full list of default modifiers provides a large set of controls for managing views:[1]

- **Text**

    - **struct Text:** A view that displays one or more lines of read-only text.

    - **struct TextField:** A control that displays an editable text interface.

---

[1] https://developer.apple.com/documentation/SwiftUI/Views-and-Controls, Apple

- **struct SecureField:** A control into which the user securely enters private text.

- **struct TextEditor:** A view that can display and edit long-form text.

- **Images**

  - **struct Image:** A view that displays an image.

  - **struct AsyncImage:** A view that asynchronously loads and displays an image.

- **Buttons**

  - **struct Button:** A control that initiates an action.

  - **struct EditButton:** A button that toggles the edit mode for the current edit scope.

  - **struct PasteButton:** A system button that reads data from the pasteboard and delivers it to a closure.

- **Controls**

  - **struct Link:** A control for navigating to a URL.

  - **struct Menu:** A control for presenting a menu of actions.

- **Value Selectors**

  - **struct Toggle:** A control that toggles between on and off states.

  - **struct Slider:** A control for selecting a value from a bounded linear range of values.

  - **struct Stepper:** A control that performs increment and decrement actions.

- **struct Picker:** A control for selecting from a set of mutually exclusive values.

- **struct DatePicker:** A control for selecting an absolute date.

- **struct ColorPicker:** A control used to select a color from the system color picker UI.

- **Value Indicators**

  - **struct Label:** A standard label for UI items, consisting of an icon with a title.

  - **struct ProgressView:** A view that shows the progress toward completion of a task.

  - **struct Gauge:** A view that shows a value within a range.

- **Localization**

  - **struct LocalizedStringKey:** The key used to lookup an entry in a strings file or strings dictionary file.

- **Infrequently Used Views**

  - **struct EmptyView:** A view that doesn't contain any content.

  - **struct EquatableView:** A view type that compares itself against its previous value and prevents its child updating if its new value is the same as its old value.

  - **struct AnyView:** A type-erased view.

  - **struct TupleView:** A View created from a swift tuple of View values.

- **Implementing a Custom View**

  - **var body: Self.Body:** The content and behavior of the view.

  - **associated type Body: View:** The type of view representing the body of this view.

  - **struct ViewBuilder:** A custom parameter attribute that constructs views from closures.

- **Implementing View Modifiers:** Bundle view modifiers that you regularly reuse into a custom view modifier:

  - **func modifier<T>(T) -> ModifiedContent<Self, T>:** Applies a modifier to a view and returns a new view.

  - **struct ModifiedContent:** A value with a modifier applied to it.

  - **struct EmptyModifier:** An empty, or identity, modifier, used during development to switch modifiers at compile time.

  - **protocol ViewModifier:** A modifier that you apply to a view or another view modifier, producing a different version of the original value.

  - **protocol EnvironmentalModifier:** A modifier that must resolve to a concrete modifier in an environment before use.

In SwiftUI, you assemble views into a hierarchy that describes your app's UI. And in order to help you customize the appearance and behavior of your app's views, you need to use view modifiers. For example, you can include modifiers to:

- add accessibility features to a view;

- adjust a view's styling, layout, and other appearance characteristics;

- respond to events, like copy and paste;

- conditionally present modal views, like popovers; and

- configure supporting views, like toolbars.

And since view modifiers are Swift methods with behavior provided by the View protocol, it is acceptable to apply them to any type that conforms to the View protocol. That includes primitive views like Text, Image, and Button, as well as views that you define.

Configuring a View with a Modifier

Like other Swift methods, a modifier operates on an instance—a view of some kind in this case—and can optionally take input parameters. For example, you can apply the foregroundColor(_:) modifier to set the color of a Text view:

```
Text("Hello, World!")
    .foregroundColor(.white) // Display
white text.
```

Modifiers return a view that wraps the original view and replaces it in the view hierarchy. You can think of the two lines in the example above as resolving to a single view that displays white text.

While the code above follows the rules of Swift, the code's structure may be unfamiliar for developers new to SwiftUI. Mainly because SwiftUI is based on a declarative approach, where you declare and configure a view at the point in your code that corresponds to the view's position in the view hierarchy. We shall cover the declarative approach in detail later in this chapter.

Chain Modifiers to Achieve Complex Effects

You commonly chain modifiers, each including the result of the previous one, by calling them one after the other. To illustrate, you can wrap a text view in an invisible box with a given width using the frame(width:height:alignment:) modifier to influence its layout, and then use the border(_:width:) modifier to draw an outline around that:

```
Text("Title")
    .frame(width: 100)
    .border(Color.gray)
```

It is also important to remember that the order in which you apply modifiers matters. For example, the border that results from the code above outlines the full width of the frame. By specifying the frame modifier after the border modifier, SwiftUI includes the border only to the text view, which never takes more space than it needs to render its content:

```
Text("Title")
    .border(Color.gray) // Apply the border
first this time.
    .frame(width: 100)
```

Wrapping that view in an invisible one with a fixed 100 points width will definitely affect the layout of the composite view but shall not have any effect on the border.

Configuring Child Views

It is possible to apply any view modifier determined by the View protocol to any concrete view, even when the modifier does not have an instant effect on its target view. The effects of a modifier shall be passed to child views that do not explicitly override the modifier.

Take a look at the example below, a VStack instance normally acts on its own only to vertically stack other views—it does not have any text to display. Therefore, applying a font(_:) modifier to the stack will have no effect on the stack. But the font modifier does apply to any of the stack's child views, some of which might display text. You can, therefore, locally override the stack's modifier by adding another to a specific child view:

```
VStack {
    Text("Title")
        .font(.title) // Override the font
of this view.
    Text("First body line.")
    Text("Second body line.")
}
.font(.body) // Set a default font for
text in the stack.
```

Using View-Specific Modifiers

While many view types rely on standard view modifiers for customization and control, some views add modifiers that are specific to that view type. You cannot use such a modifier on anything but the suitable kind of view. For instance, Text defines the bold() modifier as a convenience for introducing a bold effect to the view's text. While you can use font(_:) on any view because it is a component of the View protocol, you can use bold() only on Text views. As a result, you cannot apply it on a container view:

```
VStack {
    Text("Hello, world!")
}
.bold() // Fails because 'VStack' doesn't
have a 'bold' modifier.
```

You also will not be authorized to use it on a Text view after applying another general modifier because general modifiers return an opaque type. For example, the return value from the padding modifier is not Text, but rather an opaque result type that cannot hold a bold modifier:

```
Text("Hello, world!")
    .padding()
    .bold() // Fails because 'some View'
doesn't have a 'bold' modifier.
```

Instead, it is suggested to apply the bold modifier directly to the Text view and then add the padding in the following way:

```
Text("Hello, world!")
    .bold() // Succeeds.
    .padding()
```

List View

List view is a rather straightforward and impactful format. It could represent a container that presents rows of data organized in a single column, optionally providing the ability to choose one or more items. You can use it similarly to other SwiftUI views. The standard List view Declaration goes like this:

```
struct List<SelectionValue, Content> where
SelectionValue: Hashable, Content: View
```

List is the essential view for many apps. It would be very hard to think of an app that does not use a list view anywhere in the view hierarchy. In this chapter's "Creating Custom Views and Lists" section, we will learn how to use the list view in SwiftUI and master its features.

EXPLORING TEXT AND DECORATION

Text is another view type that displays one or more lines of read-only text. A text view draws a string in your app's UI using a body font that is suitable for the current platform. Then you can select from the variety of standard fonts, like title or caption, using the font(_:) view modifier. To illustrate with example:[2]

```
Text("Hamlet")
    .font(.title)
```

As a result, you will get a text view displaying the name "Hamlet" in a title.

---

[2] https://developer.apple.com/documentation/swiftui/text, Apple

In case you want to have more control over the styling of the text, you can use the same modifier to modify a system font or choose a custom font. You can also apply view modifiers like bold() or italic() to further style the formatting:

```
Text("by William Shakespeare")
     .font(.system(size: 12, weight: .light,
design: .serif))
     .italic()
```

In order to complete styling within specific portions of the text, you can create the text view from an AttributedString, which will let you to use Markdown to style runs of text. Meaning that you will be able to mix string attributes and SwiftUI modifiers, with the string attributes taking priority:

```
let attributedString = try!
AttributedString(
     markdown: "_Hamlet_ by William
Shakespeare")
var body: some View {
    Text(attributedString)
         .font(.system(size: 12, weight:
.light, design: .serif))
}
```

A text view is set to utilize exactly the amount of space it needs to present its rendered contents, but you can affect the view's layout. For instance, you can use the frame(width:height:alignment:) modifier to suggest specific dimensions to the view. If the view accepts the proposal but the text does not fit into the available space, the view uses a combination of wrapping, tightening, scaling, and truncation to make it fit. With a width of 100 points but no constraint on the height, a text view might wrap a long string:

```
Text("Listen to many, speak to a few:")
    .frame(width: 100)
```

You can then use modifiers like lineLimit(_:), allowsTightening(_:), minimumScaleFactor(_:), and truncationMode(_:) to set how the view shall manage space constraints. For instance, combining a fixed width and a line limit of 1 results in truncation for a text that does not fit in that space:

```
Text("There is nothing either good or bad
but thinking makes it so.")
    .frame(width: 100)
    .lineLimit(1)
```

Localizing Strings

When you initialize a text view with a string literal, the view automatically uses the init(_:tableName:bundle:comment:) initializer, which interprets the string as a localization key and searches for the key in the table you specify, or in the default table in case you do not identify any.

```
Text("book") // Searches the default table
in the main bundle.
```

For an app localized in both English and French, the above view displays "book" and "livre" for English and French users, respectively. In case the view cannot perform localization, it presents the key instead. For example, if the same app lacks Russian localization, the view displays "book" for users in that locale. Similarly, an app that lacks any localization information displays "book" in any locale.

In addition, to explicitly bypass localization for a string literal, you can use the init(verbatim:) initializer:

```
Text(verbatim: "book") // Displays the
string "book" in any locale.
```

If you initialize a text view with a variable value, the view uses the init(_:) initializer, which does not localize the string. However, you can request localization by creating a LocalizedStringKey instance first, which activates the init(_:tableName:bundle:comment:) initializer instead:

```
// Do not localize a string variable…
Text(writingImplement)
// …unless you explicitly convert it to a
localized string key.
Text(LocalizedStringKey(writingImplement))
```

When localizing a string variable, you can use the following default table by omitting the optional initialization parameters—as in the above example—just like you might for a string literal:

- **Creating a Text View from a String**

  - **init(LocalizedStringKey, tableName: String?, bundle: Bundle?, comment: StaticString?):** Creates a text view that displays localized content identified by a key.

- **init<S>(S):** Creates a text view that displays a stored string without localization.

- **init(verbatim: String):** Creates a text view that displays a string literal without localization.

- **Creating a Text View from an Attributed String**

  - **init(AttributedString):** Creates a text view that displays styled attributed content.

  - **struct LineStyle:** Description of the style used to draw the line for StrikethroughStyleAttribute and UnderlineStyleAttribute.

- **Creating a Text View for a Date**

  - **init(ClosedRange<Date>):** Creates an instance that displays a localized range between two dates.

  - **init(DateInterval):** Creates an instance that displays a localized time interval.

  - **init(Date, style: Text.DateStyle):** Creates an instance that displays localized dates and times using a specific style.

  - **struct DateStyle:** A predefined style used to display a Date.

- **Creating a Text View with Formatting**

  - **init<Subject>(Subject, formatter: Formatter):** Creates a text view that displays the formatted representation of a value.

- **init<Subject>(Subject, formatter: Formatter):** Creates a text view that displays the formatted representation of a value.

- **init<F>(F.FormatInput, format: F):** Creates a text view that displays the formatted representation of a value.

- **Creating a Text View from an Image**

  - **init(Image):** Creates an instance that wraps an Image, suitable for concatenating with other Text.

- **Choosing a Font**

  - **func font(Font?) -> Text:** Sets the default font for text in the view.

  - **func fontWeight(Font.Weight?) -> Text:** Sets the font weight of the text.

  - **struct Font:** An environment-dependent font.

- **Styling the View's Text**

  - **func foregroundColor(Color?) -> Text:** Sets the color of the text displayed by this view.

  - **func bold() -> Text:** Applies a bold font-weight to the text.

  - **func italic() -> Text:** Applies italics to the text.

  - **func strikethrough(Bool, color: Color?) -> Text:** Applies a strikethrough to the text.

  - **func underline(Bool, color: Color?) -> Text:** Applies an underline to the text.

- **func monospacedDigit() -> Text:** Applies monospaced digits feature to the text.

- **func kerning(CGFloat) -> Text:** Sets the spacing, or kerning, between characters.

- **func tracking(CGFloat) -> Text:** Sets the tracking for the text.

- **func baselineOffset(CGFloat) -> Text:** Sets the vertical offset for the text relative to its baseline.

- **func textCase(Text.Case?) -> some View:** Sets a transform for the case of the text contained in this view when displayed.

- **enum Case:** A scheme for transforming the capitalization of characters within text.

- **Fitting Text into Available Space**

  - **func allowsTightening(Bool) -> some View:** Sets whether text in this view can compress the space between characters when necessary to fit text in a line.

  - **func minimumScaleFactor(CGFloat) -> some View:** Sets the minimum amount that text in this view scales down to fit in the available space.

  - **func truncationMode(Text.TruncationMode) -> some View:** Sets the truncation mode for lines of text that are too long to fit in the available space.

  - **enum TruncationMode:** The type of truncation to apply to a line of text when it's too long to fit in the available space.

- **Handling Multiline Text**

  - **func lineLimit(Int?) -> some View:** Sets the maximum number of lines that text can occupy in this view.

  - **func lineSpacing(CGFloat) -> some View:** Sets the amount of space between lines of text in this view.

  - **func multilineTextAlignment(TextAlignment) -> some View:** Sets the alignment of multiline text in this view.

  - **enum TextAlignment:** Aligns the child view within its bounds given anchor types.

- **Controlling the Layout Direction**

  - **func flipsForRightToLeftLayoutDirection(Bool) -> some View:** Sets whether this view flips its contents horizontally when the layout direction is right-to-left.

- **Configuring VoiceOver**

  - **func speechAdjustedPitch(Double) -> Text:** Raises or lowers the pitch of spoken text.

  - **func speechAlwaysIncludesPunctuation(Bool) -> Text:** Sets whether VoiceOver should always speak all punctuation in the text view.

  - **func speechAnnouncementsQueued(Bool) -> Text:** Controls whether to queue pending announcements behind existing speech rather than interrupting speech in progress.

- **func speechSpellsOutCharacters(Bool) -> Text:** Sets whether VoiceOver should speak the contents of the text view character by character.

- **Providing Accessibility Information**

  - **func accessibilityHeading(AccessibilityHeadingLevel) -> Text:** Sets the accessibility level of this heading.

  - **func accessibilityLabel<S>(S) -> Text:** Adds a label to the view that describes its contents.

  - **func accessibilityLabel(Text) -> Text:** Adds a label to the view that describes its contents.

  - **func accessibilityLabel(LocalizedStringKey) -> Text:** Adds a label to the view that describes its contents.

  - **func accessibilityTextContentType(AccessibilityTextContentType) -> Text:** Sets an accessibility text content type.

- **Combining Text Views**

  - **static func + (Text, Text) -> Text:** Concatenates the text in two text views in a new text view.

- **Comparing Text Views**

  - **static func == (Text, Text) -> Bool:** Indicates whether two text views are equal.

  - **static func != (Self, Self) -> Bool:** Indicates whether two text views aren't equal.

CREATING CUSTOM VIEWS AND LISTS

As previously mentioned, SwiftUI offers a declarative approach to UI design. With a traditional imperative approach, the burden typically falls on your controller code not only to instantiate, layout, and configure views, but also to constantly make updates as the situation evolves. In contrast, with a declarative approach, you state a lightweight description of your UI by stating views in a hierarchy that reflects the preferred layout of your interface. SwiftUI then manages drawing and updating these views in response to events like user input or state changes.

SwiftUI offers tools for defining and modifying the views in your UI. You compose custom views out of primitive views that SwiftUI provides, plus other composite views that you might have already defined. You configure these views with view modifiers and connect them to your data model. You should then place your custom views within your app's view hierarchy.

Conforming to the View Protocol

You re expected to declare a custom view type by defining a structure that conforms to the following View protocol:

```
struct MyView: View {
}
```

Like other Swift protocols, the View protocol has a blueprint for functionality—in this case, the behavior of a component that SwiftUI draws onscreen. Conformance to the protocol comes with both requirements that a view must meet, and functionality that the protocol provides.

After you fulfill the requirements, you can add your custom view into a view hierarchy so that it becomes part of your app's UI.

Declaring a Body

One of the View protocol's main requirements is that conforming types properly defines the following body computed property:

```
struct MyView: View {
    var body: some View {
    }
}
```

SwiftUI will go back to the value of this property every time it needs to update the view, which can happen multiple times during the life of the view, potentially in response to user input or system events. The value that the view returns is an element that SwiftUI takes onscreen.

The View protocol's other requirement is that conforming types indicate an associated type for the body property. Nevertheless, there is no need to make an explicit declaration. Instead, you should declare the body property as an opaque type, using the same View syntax, to mark only that the body's type conforms to View. The exact type depends on the body's content, which changes as you edit the body during development. Swift typically infers the exact type automatically on its own.

Assembling the View's Content

If you want to further describe your view's appearance, you can do so by adding content to the view's body properly.

You can build the body from primitive views that SwiftUI provides and custom views that you have inserted elsewhere. For instance, you can create a body that draws the string "Hello, World!" using the following built-in Text view:

```
struct MyView: View {
    var body: some View {
        Text("Hello, World!")
    }
}
```

In addition to views for specific kinds of content, controls, and indicators, like Text, Toggle, and ProgressView, SwiftUI also offers primitive views that you can apply to arrange other views. For example, you can vertically stack two Text views using this VStack:

```
struct MyView: View {
    var body: some View {
        VStack {
            Text("Hello, World!")
            Text("Glad to meet you.")
        }
    }
}
```

Views that take multiple input child views, like the stack in the example above, typically do so using a closure marked by the ViewBuilder attribute. This enables a multiple-statement closure that does not take additional syntax at the call site. You would only need to list the input views in succession.

Configuring Views with Modifiers

In order to properly configure the views in your view's body, you need to apply view modifiers. Again, a modifier stands for a particular method called on a specific view. The method returns a new, altered view that would then take the place of the original in the view hierarchy.

SwiftUI has a great View protocol with an extensive set of methods. All View protocol conformers—both primitive and custom views—have access to these methods that advance the behavior of a view in some way. To demonstrate, you can modify the font of a text view by applying the following font(_:) modifier:

```swift
struct MyView: View {
    var body: some View {
        VStack {
            Text("Hello, World!")
                .font(.title)
            Text("Glad to meet you.")
        }
    }
}
```

Managing Data

In order to successfully manage data, you need to supply inputs to your views, and add properties. For example, you can make the font of the "Hello, World!" string configurable:

```swift
struct MyView: View {
    let helloFont: Font
```

```
var body: some View {
    VStack {
        Text("Hello, World!")
            .font(helloFont)
        Text("Glad to meet you.")
    }
}
}
```

If an input value changes, SwiftUI observes the change and redraws only the edited parts of your interface. This might involve reinitializing your entire view, but SwiftUI shall organize that for you.

And since the system may reinitialize a view at any time, it is important to avoid doing any significant work in your view's initialization code. It is often advised to omit an explicit initializer, therefore allowing Swift to synthesize a member-wise initializer instead.

Adding Your View to the View Hierarchy

Once you are done defining a view, you can incorporate it into other types of views, just like you do with primitive views. You add your view by declaring it at the point in the hierarchy at which you want it to appear. For example, you could put MyView in your app's ContentView, which Xcode creates automatically as the root view of a new app:

```
struct ContentView: View {
    var body: some View {
        MyView(helloFont: .title)
    }
}
```

Alternatively, you could insert your view as the root view of a new scene in your app, like the Settings scene that declares content for a macOS preferences window, or a NotificationScene scene that declares the content for a watchOS notification.

Creating and Modifying List View

In its simplest form, a List creates its contents statically, as shown in the example below:

```
var body: some View {
    List {
        Text("A-List Item")
        Text("A Second List Item")
        Text("A Third List Item")
    }
}
```

More commonly, you create lists dynamically from an underlying collection of data. The following example shows how to make a simple list from an array of an Ocean type which conforms to Identifiable:[3]

```
struct Ocean: Identifiable {
    let name: String
    let id = UUID()
}
private var oceans = [
    Ocean(name: "Pacific"),
    Ocean(name: "Atlantic"),
```

---

[3] https://developer.apple.com/documentation/swiftui/list, Apple

```
    Ocean(name: "Indian"),
    Ocean(name: "Southern"),
    Ocean(name: "Arctic")
]

var body: some View {
    List(oceans) {
        Text($0.name)
    }
}
```

Supporting Selection in Lists

To make members of a list selectable, provide a binding
to a selection variable. Binding to a single instance of the
lost data's Identifiable.ID type creates a single-selection
list. Binding to a Set creates a list that supports multiple
selections. The following example shows how to add multi-
select to the previous example. A Text view below the list
shows the number of items currently selected.

```
struct Ocean: Identifiable, Hashable {
    let name: String
    let id = UUID()
}
private var oceans = [
    Ocean(name: "Pacific"),
    Ocean(name: "Atlantic"),
    Ocean(name: "Indian"),
    Ocean(name: "Southern"),
    Ocean(name: "Arctic")
]
@State private var multiSelection =
Set<UUID>()
```

```
var body: some View {
    NavigationView {
        List(oceans, selection:
$multiSelection) {
            Text($0.name)
        }
        .navigationTitle("Oceans")
        .toolbar {EditButton()}
    }
    Text("\(multiSelection.count)
selections")
}
```

Refreshing the List Content

In order to make the content of the list refreshable using the standard refresh control, you can apply the refreshable(action:) modifier.

The example below shows how to add a standard refresh control to a list. When the user drags the top of the list downward, SwiftUI reveals the refresh control and executes the specified action. You can use an await expression inside the action closure to refresh your data with the refresh indicator visible for the duration of the awaited operation:

```
struct Ocean: Identifiable, Hashable {
    let name: String
    let id = UUID()
    let stats: [String: String]
}
class OceanStore: ObservableObject {
    @Published var oceans = [Ocean]()
    func loadStats() async -> Void {}
}
```

```
@EnvironmentObject var store: OceanStore
var body: some View {
    NavigationView {
        List(store.oceans) { ocean in
            HStack {
                Text(ocean.name)
                StatsSummary(stats: ocean.
stats) // A custom view for showing
statistics.
            }
        }
        .refreshable {
            await store.loadStats()
        }
        .navigationTitle("Oceans")
    }
}
```

Supporting Multidimensional Lists

To be able to support two-dimensional lists, your list's content should include instances of the Section type, which then provide their own contents.

The following example illustrates sections named after the world's oceans, each of which has Text children named for major seas attached to those oceans. The example also allows for selection of a single list item, identified by the id of the example's Sea type:[4]

```
struct ContentView: View {
    struct Sea: Hashable, Identifiable {
        let name: String
```

```
        let id = UUID()
    }
    struct OceanRegion: Identifiable {
        let name: String
        let seas: [Sea]
        let id = UUID()
    }
    private let oceanRegions: [OceanRegion]
= [
        OceanRegion(name: "Pacific",
                      seas: [Sea(name:
"Australasian Mediterranean"),
                            Sea(name:
"Philippine"),
                            Sea(name:
"Coral"),
                            Sea(name: "South
China")]),
        OceanRegion(name: "Atlantic",
                      seas: [Sea(name:
"American Mediterranean"),
                            Sea(name:
"Sargasso"),
                            Sea(name:
"Caribbean")]),
        OceanRegion(name: "Indian",
                      seas: [Sea(name: "Bay
of Bengal")]),
        OceanRegion(name: "Southern",
                      seas:
[Sea(name:"Weddell")]),
        OceanRegion(name: "Arctic",
```

```
                        seas: [Sea(name:
"Greenland")])
    ]
    @State private var singleSelection :
UUID?

    var body: some View {
        NavigationView {
            List(selection:
$singleSelection){
                ForEach(oceanRegions) {
region in
                    Section(header:
Text("Major \(region.name) Ocean Seas")) {
                        ForEach(region
.seas) { sea in
                            Text(sea.name)
                        }
                    }
                }
            }
            .navigationTitle("Oceans and
Seas")
            .toolbar { EditButton() }
        }
    }
}
```

Creating Hierarchical Lists

It is also possible to create a hierarchical list of arbitrary depth by providing tree-structured data and a children parameter that has a key path to gather the child nodes at any level. The following example demonstrates how to script a deeply-nested collection of a custom FileItem type to simulate the contents of a file system. The list created from this data applies collapsing cells to let the user navigate the tree structure:[5]

```swift
struct ContentView: View {
    struct FileItem: Hashable,
Identifiable, CustomStringConvertible {
        var id: Self { self }
        var name: String
        var children: [FileItem]? = nil
        var description: String {
            switch children {
            case nil:
                return "■ \(name)"
            case .some(let children):
                return children.isEmpty ?
"📁 \(name)" : "📁 \(name)"
            }
        }
    }
    let fileHierarchyData: [FileItem] = [
      FileItem(name: "users", children:
        [FileItem(name: "user1234",
children:
            [FileItem(name: "Photos",
children:
```

[5] https://developer.apple.com/documentation/swiftui/list, Apple

```
                [FileItem(name: "photo001.
jpg"),
                 FileItem(name: "photo002.
jpg")]),
            FileItem(name: "Movies",
children:
                [FileItem(name: "movie001.
mp4")]),
                FileItem(name: "Documents",
children: [])
            ]),
        FileItem(name: "newuser",
children:
            [FileItem(name: "Documents",
children: [])
            ])
        ]),
        FileItem(name: "private", children:
nil)
    ]
    var body: some View {
        List(fileHierarchyData, children:
\.children) { item in
            Text(item.description)
        }
    }
}
```

Styling Lists

When it comes to styling lists, SwiftUI opts for a display style for a list based on the platform and the view type in which it appears. You can use the listStyle(_:) modifier to apply a different ListStyle to all lists within a view or you can select other options from the following variety:[6]

- **Creating a List with Arbitrary Content**

  - **init(content: () -> Content):** Creates a list with the given content.

  - **init(selection: Binding<SelectionValue?>?, content: () -> Content):** Creates a list with the given content that supports selecting a single row.

  - **init(selection: Binding<Set<SelectionValue>>?, content: () -> Content):** Creates a list with the given content that supports selecting multiple rows.

- **Creating a List from a Range**

  - **init<RowContent>(Range<Int>, rowContent: (Int) -> RowContent):** Creates a list that computes its views on demand over a constant range.

  - **init<RowContent>(Range<Int>, selection: Binding<SelectionValue?>?, rowContent: (Int) -> RowContent):** Creates a list that computes its views on demand over a constant range, optionally allowing users to select a single row.

  - **init<RowContent>(Range<Int>, selection: Binding<Set<SelectionValue>>?, rowContent: (Int) -> RowContent):** Creates a list that computes its views on demand over a constant range, optionally allowing users to select multiple rows.

---

[6] https://developer.apple.com/documentation/swiftui/list, Apple

- **Creating a List from Identifiable Data**

  - **init<Data, RowContent>(Data, rowContent: (Data.Element) -> RowContent):** Creates a list that computes its rows on demand from an underlying collection of identifiable data.

  - **init<Data, RowContent>(Data, selection: Binding<SelectionValue?>?, rowContent: (Data. Element) -> RowContent):** Creates a list that computes its rows on demand from an underlying collection of identifiable data, optionally allowing users to select a single row.

  - **init<Data, RowContent>(Data, selection: Binding<Set<SelectionValue>>?, rowContent: (Data.Element) -> RowContent):** Creates a list that computes its rows on demand from an underlying collection of identifiable data, optionally allowing users to select multiple rows.

- **Creating a List from Data and an Identifier**

  - **init<Data, ID, RowContent>(Data, id: KeyPath<Data.Element, ID>, rowContent: (Data. Element) –> RowContent):** Creates a list that identifies its rows based on a key path to the identifier of the underlying data.

  - **init<Data, ID, RowContent>(Data, id: KeyPath<Data.Element, ID>, selection: Binding<SelectionValue?>?, rowContent: (Data.Element) -> RowContent):** Creates a list that identifies its rows based on a key path to the identifier of the underlying data, optionally allowing users to select a single row.

- **init<Data, ID, RowContent>(Data, id: KeyPath<Data.Element, ID>, selection: Binding<Set<SelectionValue>>?, rowContent: (Data.Element) -> RowContent):** Creates a list that identifies its rows based on a key path to the identifier of the underlying data, optionally allowing users to select multiple rows.

- **Creating a List from a Binding to Identifiable Data**

  - **init<Data, RowContent>(Binding<Data>, rowContent: (Binding<Data.Element>) -> RowContent):** Creates a list that computes its rows on demand from an underlying collection of identifiable data.

  - **init<Data, RowContent>(Binding<Data>, selection: Binding<SelectionValue?>?, rowContent: (Binding<Data.Element>) -> RowContent):** Creates a list that computes its rows on demand from an underlying collection of identifiable data, optionally allowing users to select a single row.

  - **init<Data, RowContent>(Binding<Data>, selection: Binding<Set<SelectionValue>>?, rowContent: (Binding<Data.Element>) -> RowContent):** Creates a list that computes its rows on demand from an underlying collection of identifiable data, optionally allowing users to select multiple rows.

- **Creating a List from a Binding to Data and an Identifier**

  - **init<Data, ID, RowContent>(Binding<Data>, id: KeyPath<Data.Element, ID>, rowContent: (Binding<Data.Element>) -> RowContent):**

Creates a list that identifies its rows based on a key path to the identifier of the underlying data. Available when SelectionValue is Never and Content conforms to View.

- **init<Data, ID, RowContent>(Binding<Data>, id: KeyPath<Data.Element, ID>, selection: Binding<SelectionValue?>?, rowContent: (Binding<Data.Element>) -> RowContent):** Creates a list that identifies its rows based on a key path to the identifier of the underlying data, optionally allowing users to select a single row. Available when SelectionValue conforms to Hashable and Content conforms to View.

- **init<Data, ID, RowContent>(Binding<Data>, id: KeyPath<Data.Element, ID>, selection: Binding<Set<SelectionValue>>?, rowContent: (Binding<Data.Element>) -> RowContent):** Creates a list that identifies its rows based on a key path to the identifier of the underlying data, optionally allowing users to select multiple rows. Available when SelectionValue conforms to Hashable and Content conforms to View.

- **Creating a List from Hierarchical, Identifiable Data**

  - **init<Data, RowContent>(Data, children: KeyPath<Data.Element, Data?>, rowContent: (Data.Element) -> RowContent):** Creates a hierarchical list that computes its rows on demand from an underlying collection of identifiable data. Available when SelectionValue is Never and Content conforms to View.

- **init<Data, RowContent>(Data, children: Key Path<Data.Element, Data?>, selection: Binding-<SelectionValue?>?,rowContent:(Data.Element)-> RowContent):** Creates a hierarchical list that computes its rows on demand from an underlying collection of identifiable data, optionally allowing users to select a single row. Available when SelectionValue conforms to Hashable and Content conforms to View.

- **init<Data, RowContent>(Data, children: KeyPath<Data.Element, Data?>, selection: Binding<Set<SelectionValue>>?, rowContent: (Data.Element) -> RowContent):** Creates a hierarchical list that computes its rows on demand from an underlying collection of identifiable data, optionally allowing users to select multiple rows. Available when SelectionValue conforms to Hashable and Content conforms to View.

- **Creating a List from Hierarchical Data and an Identifier**

  - **init<Data, ID, RowContent>(Data, id: KeyPath-<Data.Element, ID>, children: KeyPath<Data. Element, Data?>, rowContent: (Data.Element) -> RowContent):** Creates a hierarchical list that identifies its rows based on a key path to the identifier of the underlying data. Available when SelectionValue is Never and Content conforms to View.

  - **init<Data, ID, RowContent>(Data, id: Key Path<Data.Element, ID>, children: KeyPath<**

Data.Element, Data?>, selection: Binding< SelectionValue?>?, rowContent: (Data.Element) -> RowContent): Creates a hierarchical list that identifies its rows based on a key path to the identifier of the underlying data, optionally allowing users to select a single row. Available when SelectionValue conforms to Hashable and Content conforms to View.

- **init<Data, ID, RowContent>(Data, id: KeyPath< Data.Element, ID>, children: KeyPath<Data. Element, Data?>, selection: Binding<Set<Select ionValue>>?, rowContent: (Data.Element) -> RowContent):** Creates a hierarchical list that identifies its rows based on a key path to the identifier of the underlying data, optionally allowing users to select multiple rows. Available when SelectionValue conforms to Hashable and Content conforms to View.

- **Creating a List from a Binding to Hierarchical, Identifiable Data**

  - **init<Data, RowContent>(Binding<Data>, children: WritableKeyPath<Data.Element, Data?>, rowContent: (Binding<Data.Element>) -> RowContent):** Creates a hierarchical list that computes its rows on demand from a binding to an underlying collection of identifiable data. Available when SelectionValue is Never and Content conforms to View.

  - **init<Data, RowContent>(Binding<Data>, children: WritableKeyPath<Data.Element, Data?>,**

selection: Binding<SelectionValue?>?, rowContent: (Binding<Data.Element>) -> RowContent):
Creates a hierarchical list that computes its rows on demand from a binding to an underlying collection of identifiable data, optionally allowing users to select a single row. Available when SelectionValue conforms to Hashable and Content conforms to View.

- **init<Data, RowContent>(Binding<Data>, children: WritableKeyPath<Data.Element, Data?>, selection: Binding<Set<SelectionValue>>?, rowContent: (Binding<Data.Element>) -> RowContent):** Creates a hierarchical list that computes its rows on demand from a binding to an underlying collection of identifiable data, optionally allowing users to select multiple rows. Available when SelectionValue conforms to Hashable and Content conforms to View.

- **Creating a List from a Binding to Hierarchical Data and an Identifier**

  - **init<Data, ID, RowContent>(Binding<Data>, id: KeyPath<Data.Element, ID>, children: WritableKeyPath<Data.Element, Data?>, rowContent: (Binding<Data.Element>) -> RowContent):** Creates a hierarchical list that identifies its rows based on a key path to the identifier of the underlying data. Available when SelectionValue is Never and Content conforms to View.

  - **init<Data, ID, RowContent>(Binding<Data>, id: KeyPath<Data.Element, ID>, children:**

WritableKeyPath<Data.Element, Data?>, selection: Binding<SelectionValue?>?, rowContent: (Binding<Data.Element>) -> RowContent): Creates a hierarchical list that identifies its rows based on a key path to the identifier of the underlying data, optionally allowing users to select a single row. Available when SelectionValue conforms to Hashable and Content conforms to View.

- **init<Data, ID, RowContent>(Binding<Data>, id: KeyPath<Data.Element, ID>, children: WritableKeyPath<Data.Element, Data?>, selection: Binding<Set<SelectionValue>>?, rowContent: (Binding<Data.Element>) -> RowContent):** Creates a hierarchical list that identifies its rows based on a key path to the identifier of the underlying data, optionally allowing users to select multiple rows. Available when SelectionValue conforms to Hashable and Content conforms to View.

- **Styling Lists**

  - **func listStyle<S>(S) -> some View:** Sets the style for lists within this view.

  - **protocol ListStyle:** A protocol that describes the behavior and appearance of a list.

DECLARATIVE SYNTAX

Like Java, C++, PHP, and C#, Swift has been designed as an imperative programming language. SwiftUI, however, is claimed as a declarative UI framework that offers developers a chance to create UI in a declarative way. Yet what does the term "declarative" mean and how does it differ from imperative programming? Most importantly, how does this change affect the way you are going to approach coding?

If you are new to programming, you probably do not need to focus on the difference since everything would be new to you anyway. However, if you have previously experienced Object-oriented programming or developed with UIKit, this method shift might affect how you think about building a UI. You simply might be forced to unlearn some old patterns and relearn the new ones.

So, what's the difference between imperative and declarative programming? To put it simply, imperative programming is a programming paradigm that utilizes statements that affect a program's state. In much the same way that the imperative setup in natural languages delivers commands, an imperative program holds various commands for the computer to complete. On the other hand, declarative programming follows a different style of building the structure and elements of computer programs—it expresses the logic of a computation without outlining its control flow.

It could be challenging to understand the actual difference if you do not have a basic background in Computer Science. Let us explain the difference this way. Instead of focusing on programming, we shall talk about baking an apple pie. Assuming you ask someone to prepare an apple pie for you, you can either do it imperatively or declaratively. In order to bake the pie imperatively, you deliver each of the instructions clearly like a recipe:

- Heat the oven to 450°F or higher for at least 20 minutes

- Prepare one pound of dough

- Roll out the dough to make a 10-inch circle

- Spoon the apple jam onto the center and spread it out to the edges

- Bake the pie for 15 minutes

On the other hand, if you bake it in a declarative way, you do not need to specify the step-by-step instructions but just state how you would like the pie cooked. Thick or thin crust? 10-inch or 16-inch? The chef will have to figure out the rest and bake the pie for you.

That is the key difference between the term imperative and declarative. Imperative UI programming requires developers to provide detailed instructions to layout the UI and control its states. Conversely, declarative UI programming lets developers describe how the UI looks like and what you want to do when a state changes. The declarative way of coding style would make the code easier to read and understand. Most importantly, the SwiftUI framework lets you write way less code to create a UI.

Now let us switch from metaphors to code. Below you can analyze the same function but with imperative implementation first and the declarative implementation second.

Imperative implementation:

```
func filter(array: [Person], name: String)
-> [Person] {
  var result = [Person]()
  for item in array {
    if item.name == name {
      result.append(item)
```

```
    }
  }
  return result
}
```

Declarative implementation:

```
func filter(array: [Person], name: String)
-> [Person] {
  return array.filter({ $0.name == name })
}
```

As you might have noticed, in the declarative implementation we do not care how the filter is set we are just asking the higher-order function to give us all persons with a specific name, while in the imperative way, you have an array where you check for each item name then append that item to the array if true or else you ignore it.

SwiftUI is unarguably still quite new. It will take some time to grow into a mature framework, but what is clear already now is that SwiftUI is the future of application development for Apple platforms. Even though it may not be applicable to your production projects, it is recommended to start a side project just to explore the potential of the framework. Once you try out SwiftUI and master the skills, you will enjoy developing UI in a declarative way. In the next chapter, we shall look into the Machine Learning potential of Swift, review its essential elements and detect objects by Core ML and Vision.

CHAPTER 7

Machine Learning on Swift

IN THIS CHAPTER

➢ Learning about Core ML

➢ Configuring Machine Learning APIs

➢ Figuring how to detect objects using Core ML and Vision

The preceding chapter mainly was dedicated to the building blocks of SwiftUI. But the last chapter shall cover possibilities of Machine Learning on Swift. Machine learning as a field promises to gain increased intelligence to the software by enabling us to learn and process information efficiently and discover certain patterns that are otherwise unattainable. This chapter will hopefully inspire you to take

DOI: 10.1201/9781003254089-7

on an exciting journey in machine learning using the popular Swift language.

In the first part of this chapter, we'll start with machine learning basics to develop a lasting impression of fundamental machine learning concepts. We explore various supervised and unsupervised techniques and how to implement them in Swift. The last section will dive into some hardcore topics such as visual compression and GPU acceleration and provide some recommendations to avoid common mistakes during machine learning application development.

In case you are new to machine learning, it is better to start by demystifying some common terms:

- Artificial Intelligence (AI) is the capacity added to a machine programmatically to mimic human actions and thoughts.

- Machine Learning (ML) is a subset of AI that trains machines to complete certain tasks. For instance, you can use ML to train a machine to recognize a person in an image or translate text from one language to another.

- Deep Learning is one method of training a machine. This technique imitates the human brain, which consists of neurons located in a network. Deep Learning trains an artificial neural network from the data provided.

Apple released Core ML and Vision framework in iOS 11. Core ML allows developers to bring machine learning models into their apps. This makes it possible to include intelligent features on-device like object detection. Later, iOS 13 added on-device training in Core ML 3 and introduced new ways to personalize the user experience. In the next few chapters, you will learn how to fine-tune a model on the device using Core ML and Vision.

CORE ML

Core ML is Apple's machine learning framework that enables developers to utilize powerful ML models on-device by taking full advantage of a great variety of model types. Core ML is optimized for on-device performance by leveraging Apple hardware and limiting memory footprint and power consumption. Some of the most popular features include the following:

- **Runs models fully on-device:** Core ML models run strictly on the user's device and remove any need for a network connection, maintaining your app responsive and your users' data private.

- **Runs advanced neural networks:** Core ML supports the latest models, such as cutting-edge neural networks produced to understand images, video, sound, and other multimedia.

- **Deploys models:** With Core ML Model Deployment, you can easily share models to your app using CloudKit.

- **Converts models to Core ML:** Models from popular libraries such as TensorFlow or PyTorch can be converted to Core ML using Core ML Converters.

- **Personalizes models on-device:** Models inserted in apps can be updated with user data on-device, allowing models to stay relevant to user behavior without compromising privacy.

- **Encrypts models:** Xcode supports model encryption enabling an extra layer of security for your machine learning models.

Core ML is the widely applied way to integrate machine learning models into your app. Not only it provides a unified representation for all models, it can also train or fine-tune models on the user's device.

A model could be viewed as the result of applying a machine-learning algorithm to a set of training data. You use a model to make predictions based on new input data. Models can perform a wide variety of tasks that would be complicated or impractical to script in code. For instance, you can train a model to categorize photos or detect specific objects within a photo directly from its pixels.

Additionally, it is possible to build and train a model with the Create ML app that comes with Xcode. Alternatively, you can use a wide variety of machine learning libraries and then applyCore ML Tools to convert the model into the Core ML format. If a model is on a user's device, you can use Core ML to retrain or fine-tune it on-device, with that user's data.

Therefore, Core ML could be regarded as the foundation for domain-specific frameworks and functionality. Core ML supports Vision for analyzing images, Natural Language for processing text, Speech for converting audio to primitives like Accelerate and Metal Performance Shaders.

Create ML has a variety of model types to choose from. Just select a model type in the app and add your data and parameters to start training:

- **Image**
  - Image classification
  - Object detection
  - Hand pose classification
  - Style transfer
- **Video**
  - Action classification
  - Hand action classification
  - Style transfer
- **Motion**
  - Activity classification
- **Sound**
  - Sound classification
- **Text**
  - Text classification
  - Word tagging
- **Tabular**
  - Tabular classification
  - Tabular regression

While creating Core ML models you can also complete the following essential activities in the meantime:

- **Multimodel training:** With Core ML you can train multiple models using different datasets, all in a single project.

- **Model previews:** The framework allows you to preview your model performance using Continuity with your iPhone camera and microphone on your Mac, or drop in sample data.

- **Training control:** You are free to pause, save, resume, and extend your training process.

- **On-device training:** It is possible to train models fast right on your Mac while taking advantage of CPU and GPU. Also, you can use an external graphics processing unit with your Mac for even better model training performance.

Creating ML Framework

With Core ML framework, you can programmatically experiment and automate model creation in Swift scripts or playgrounds. It has never been easier to build dynamic app features that leverage ML train models directly from user input or on-device behavior, providing personalized and flexible experiences while prioritizing user privacy.

Moreover, you can make use of the Create ML tool on macOS playgrounds to create and train custom machine learning models. With it, you can train models to complete tasks like recognizing images, extracting meaning from text, or finding a correlation between numerical values.

You start training a model by making it recognize patterns in various representative samples. For instance, you can train a model to recognize cats by showing it lots of images of different cats. After you have trained the model, you can test it out on data it has not seen before, and evaluate how well it performed the task. When the model is performing well enough, you can integrate it into your app using Core ML.

Create ML is known to have introduced basic machine learning infrastructure into Apple products like Photos and Siri. You can start working on your image classification and natural language programming with the following key models:[1]

- **Image Models**

  - **struct MLImageClassifier:** A model you train to classify images.

  - **struct MLObjectDetector:** A model you train to classify one or more objects within an image.

  - **struct MLHandPoseClassifier:** A task that creates a hand pose classification model by training with images of people's hands that you provide.

- **Video Models**

  - **struct MLActionClassifier:** A model you train with videos to classify a person's body movements.

---

[1] https://developer.apple.com/documentation/createml, Apple

- **struct MLHandActionClassifier:** A task that creates a hand action classification model by training with videos of people's hand movements that you provide.

- **struct MLStyleTransfer:** A model you train to apply an image's style to other images or videos.

- **Text Models**

  - **struct MLTextClassifier:** A model you train to classify natural language text.

  - **struct MLWordTagger:** A word-tagging model you train to classify natural language text at the word level.

  - **struct MLGazetteer:** A collection of terms and their labels, which augments a tagger that analyzes natural language text.

  - **struct MLWordEmbedding:** A map of strings in a vector space that enable your app to find similar strings by looking at a string's neighbors.

- **Sound Models**

  - **struct MLSoundClassifier:** A machine learning model you train with audio files to recognize and identify sounds on a device.

- **Motion Models**

  - **struct MLActivityClassifier:** A model you train to classify motion sensor data.

- **Tabular Models:** Model types for general tasks, such as labeling, estimating, or finding similarities. The models learn from columns of data values in a data table.

- **enum MLClassifier:** A model you train to classify data into discrete categories.

- **enum MLRegressor:** A model you train to estimate continuous values.

- **struct MLRecommender:** A model you train to make recommendations based on item similarity, grouping, and, optionally, item ratings.

- **Model Accuracy**

  - **struct MLClassifierMetrics:** Metrics you use to evaluate a classifier's performance.

  - **struct MLRegressorMetrics:** Metrics you use to evaluate a regressor's performance.

  - **struct MLWordTaggerMetrics:** Metrics you use to evaluate a word tagger's performance.

  - **struct MLRecommenderMetrics:** Metrics you use to evaluate a recommender's performance.

  - **struct MLObjectDetectorMetrics:** Metrics you use to evaluate an object detector's performance.

- **Model Training Control**

  - **class MLJob:** The representation of a model's asynchronous training session you use to monitor the session's progress or terminate its execution.

  - **class MLTrainingSession:** The current state of a model's asynchronous training session.

- **struct MLTrainingSessionParameters:** The configuration settings for a training session.

- **struct MLCheckpoint:** The state of a model's asynchronous training session at a specific point in time during the feature extraction or training phase.

- **Supporting Types**

  - **enum MLCreateError:** The errors Create ML throws while performing various operations, such as training models, making predictions, writing models to a file system, and so on.

  - **struct MLModelMetadata:** Information about a model that's stored in a Core ML model file.

  - **enum MLSplitStrategy:** Data partitioning approaches, typically for creating a validation dataset from a training dataset.

MACHINE LEARNING APIs

Machine Learning Application Programming Interface (API) is responsible for orderly bringing all of the on-device machine learning features, like object detection in images and video, language analysis, and sound classification. Main categories of API include the following:

- **Vision:** Used to build features that can process and examine images and video using computer vision.

- **Natural Language:** Applied to review and make sense of text in various ways, like embedding or classifying words.

- **Speech:** Mostly applied to activate speech recognition and saliency features for a variety of languages.

- **Sound:** Sound features are used to analyze audio and recognize it as a particular type, such as laughter or scream.

We shall go through each of these categories one by one, leaving the biggest type, the Vision, for a separate section.

Natural Language

This API category is mainly used to complete analysis of a natural language text and deduce its language-specific metadata. The Natural Language framework provides a variety of natural language processing methods with support for many different languages. You can use this framework to divide natural language text into paragraphs, sentences, or words, and tag information about those sections, such as part of speech, lexical class, lemma, script, and language.

In addition, you can use this framework to perform the following tasks:[2]

- *Language identification*, that stands for automatically detecting the language of a piece of text

- *Tokenization* or breaking up a piece of text into linguistic units or tokens

- *Parts-of-speech tagging* or marking up individual words with their part of speech

---

[2] https://developer.apple.com/documentation/naturallanguage, Apple

- *Lemmatization* or deducing a word's stem based on its morphological analysis

- *Named entity recognition*, which is the same as identifying tokens as names of people, places, or organizations

You can also use this framework with Create ML to train and employ the following custom natural language models:[3]

- **Tokenization**

  - **class NLTokenizer:** A tokenizer that segments natural language text into semantic units.

- **Language Identification**

  - **class NLLanguageRecognizer:** The language of a body of text.

  - **struct NLLanguage:** The languages that the Natural Language framework supports.

- **Linguistic Tags**

  - **class NLTagger:** A tagger that analyzes natural language text.

- **Text Embedding**

  - **class NLEmbedding:** A map of strings to vectors, which locates neighboring, similar strings.

- **Natural Language Models**

  - **class NLModel:** A custom model trained to classify or tag natural language text.

---

[3] https://developer.apple.com/documentation/naturallanguage, Apple

Now let us demonstrate how to build and activate one of the Natural Language models related to creating a Text Classifier Model.

Creating a Text Classifier Model

A text classifier is a standard machine learning model that has been set to recognize patterns in natural language text, like the intention expressed by a sentence.

You need to train a text classifier by showing it lots of examples of text you have already processed—for example, movie reviews that you have already evaluated as positive, negative, or neutral. You can start by gathering textual data and importing it into an MLDataTable instance. You can create a data table from JSON and CSV formats. Or, if you are dealing with textual data that comes as a collection of files, you can divide them into folders, using the folder names as labels.

To illustrate with an example, take a look at the following JSON file containing movie reviews that are categorized by sentiment. Each entry holds a pair of keys, the text and the label. The values of those keys are the input samples used to train your model. The JSON snippet below has three pairs of sentences with their sentiment labels:

```
// JSON file
[
    {
        "text": "The movie was great!",
        "label": "positive"
    }, {
        "text": " The movie was quite
boring.",
```

```
        "label": "negative"
    }, {
        "text": "I was not impressed.",
        "label": "neutral"
    } ...
]
```

After that you should access the macOS playground and create the data table using the init(contentsOf:options:) method of MLDataTable:

```
import CreateML
let data = try MLDataTable(contentsOf:
URL(fileURLWithPath: "<#/path/to/read/
data.json#>"))
```

The resulting data will then be presented in two columns, named text and label, derived from the keys in the JSON file.

With that you can start to create an instance of MLTextClassifier with your training data table and the names of your columns. Training may begin with the following code:

```
let sentimentClassifier = try
MLTextClassifier(trainingData:
trainingData,
                textColumn: "text",
                labelColumn: "label")
```

During training, Create ML automatically puts aside a small percentage of the training data to use for examining the model's progress during the training phase. This examination data allows the training process to gauge the model's performance on examples the model has not been trained on. Depending on the examined accuracy, the training algorithm could adjust values within the model or even stop the training process altogether in case the accuracy is high enough. In order to see how accurately the model performed on the training and validation data, use the classificationError properties of the model's training-Metrics and validationMetrics properties:

```
// Training accuracy as a percentage
let trainingAccuracy = (1.0 -
sentimentClassifier.trainingMetrics.
classificationError) * 100

// Validation accuracy as a percentage
let validationAccuracy = (1.0 -
sentimentClassifier.validationMetrics.
classificationError) * 100
```

Next, you are expected to evaluate your trained model's performance by testing it against sentences it has never seen before. Pass your testing data table to the evaluation(on:) method, which returns an MLClassifierMetrics instance:

```
let evaluationMetrics = sentimentClassifier.
evaluation(on: testingData)
```

In case you see that your model is performing well enough, you can save it so you can use it in your app. Use the write(to:metadata:) method to write the Core ML model file (SentimentClassifier.mlmodel) to disk. Also remember to provide any information about the model, like its author, version, or description in an MLModelMetadata instance:

```
let metadata = MLModelMetadata(author:
"Dan Brown text",
                shortDescription: "A model
trained to classify movie review
sentiment",
                version: "1.0")

try sentimentClassifier.write(to:
URL(fileURLWithPath: "<#/path/to/save/
SentimentClassifier.mlmodel#>"),
                metadata: metadata)
```

Then, with your app open in Xcode, move the SentimentClassifier.mlmodel file into the navigation pane. Xcode shall automatically compile the model and generate a SentimentClassifier class for use in your app.

In addition, you can also create an NLModel in the Natural Language framework from the SentimentClassifier to make sure that the tokenization is consistent between training and deployment. In case you want to generate predictions on new text inputs you can insert the predictedLabel(for:) in your NLModel in the following manner:

```
import NaturalLanguage
import CoreML
let mlModel = try SentimentClassifier(conf
iguration: MLModelConfiguration()).model
```

```
let sentimentPredictor = try
NLModel(mlModel: mlModel)
sentimentPredictor.predictedLabel(for: "It
was great!")
```

Speech

API's Speech framework performs speech recognition on live or prerecorded audio. It is most helpful if you require transcriptions or alternative interpretations. Moreover, Speech framework's dictation support uses speech recognition to translate audio content into text.

You can complete speech recognition in many languages, but each SFSpeechRecognizer object shall operate on a single language. On-device speech recognition is available for some languages, but the framework also relies on Apple's servers for speech recognition. One should also keep in mind that performing speech recognition requires a good network connection. The following models are essential when it comes to completing speech recognition using Apple's servers:[4]

- **class SFSpeechRecognizer:** An object you use to check for the availability of the speech recognition service, and to initiate the speech recognition process.

- **Audio Sources:** Mostly used to perform speech recognition on audio coming from the microphone of an iOS device:

  - **class SFSpeechURLRecognitionRequest:** A request to recognize speech in a recorded audio file.

---

[4] https://developer.apple.com/documentation/speech, Apple

- **class SFSpeechAudioBufferRecognitionRequest:** A request to recognize speech from captured audio content, such as audio from the device's microphone.

- **class SFSpeechRecognitionRequest:** An abstract class representing a request to recognize speech from an audio source.

- **In-Progress Requests**

  - **class SFSpeechRecognitionTask:** A task object that you use to monitor the speech recognition progress.

- **Transcription Results**

  - **class SFSpeechRecognitionResult:** An object containing the partial or final results of a speech recognition request.

  - **class SFTranscription:** A textual representation of the given speech in its entirety, as recognized by the speech recognizer.

  - **class SFTranscriptionSegment:** A discrete part of an entire transcription, as identified by the speech recognizer.

Recognizing Speech in Live Audio

This section shall provide a sample demonstration on how to use the Speech framework to recognize words from captured audio. Once you tap the Start Recording button, the SpokenWord tool begins capturing audio from the device's microphone. It locates that audio to the APIs of the Speech framework, which processes the audio and sends back recognized text. The app then shall display the recognized text in its text view, continuously updating that text until you tap the Stop Recording button.

At the same time, it is important to keep in mind that the framework must include the NSSpeechRecognitionUsageDescription key in its Info. plist file and must request authorization to perform speech recognition.

Configuring the Microphone Using AVFoundation SpokenWord uses AV Foundation to connect to the device's microphone. Specifically, the app regulates the shared AVAudioSession object to manage the app's audio interactions with the rest of the system, and it modifies an AVAudioEngine object to retrieve the following microphone input:

```
private let audioEngine = AVAudioEngine()
```

Once you press the Start Recording button, the app retrieves the shared AVAudioSession object, configures it for recording, and turns it into an active session. Activating the session lets the system know that the app requires microphone resource. Once the session is active, the app obtains the AVAudioInputNode object from its audio engine and places it in the local inputNode variable. This input node stands for the current audio input path, which can be the device's built-in microphone or a microphone connected to a set of headphones.

The app has to install a tap on the input node and start up the audio engine, which collects samples into an internal buffer to begin recording. When a buffer is full, the audio engine takes on the provided block. The app's implementation of that block passes the samples directly to the request object's append(_:) method, which holds the audio samples and forwards them to the speech recognition system:

```
// Configure the microphone input.
let recordingFormat = inputNode.
outputFormat(forBus: 0)
inputNode.installTap(onBus: 0, bufferSize:
1024, format: recordingFormat) {(buffer:
AVAudioPCMBuffer, when: AVAudioTime) in
    self.recognitionRequest?.append(buffer)
}
audioEngine.prepare()
try audioEngine.start()
```

In order to recognize speech from live audio, SpokenWord creates and modifies an SFSpeechAudioBufferRecognitionRequest object. When it receives recognition results, the app updates its text view accordingly. The app sets the request object's shouldReportPartialResults property to true, which pushes the speech recognition system to return immediate results as they are recognized:

```
// Create and configure the speech
recognition request.
recognitionRequest =
SFSpeechAudioBufferRecognitionRequest()
guard let recognitionRequest =
recognitionRequest else {fatalError("Unable
to create a
SFSpeechAudioBufferRecognitionRequest
object")}
```

```
recognitionRequest.
shouldReportPartialResults = true
```

And when it comes to the speech recognition process, the app calls recognitionTask(with:resultHandler:) on its SFSpeechRecognizer object. That method applies the information in the provided request object to regulate the speech recognition system and to begin processing audio asynchronously. Right after calling it, the app starts appending audio samples to the request object. And if you tap the Stop Recording button, the app stops adding samples and ends the speech recognition procedure.

Since the request's shouldReportPartialResults property in the above example is true, the recognitionTask(with:res ultHandler:) method implements its block periodically to deliver partial results. The app uses that block to update its text view with the text in the bestTranscription property of the result object. And in case it receives an error instead of a result, the app stops the recognition process altogether in the following manner:

```
5// Create a recognition task for the
speech recognition session.
// Keep a reference to the task so that it
can be canceled.
recognitionTask = speechRecognizer.
recognitionTask(with: recognitionRequest)
{result, error in
    var isFinal = false
```

---

5 https://developer.apple.com/documentation/speech/recognizing_speech_
in_live_audio, Apple

```
    if let result = result {
        // Update the text view with the
results.
        self.textView.text = result.
bestTranscription.formattedString
        isFinal = result.isFinal
        print("Text\(result.
bestTranscription.formattedString)")
    }

    if error != nil || isFinal {
        // Stop recognizing speech if there
is a problem.
        self.audioEngine.stop()
        inputNode.removeTap(onBus: 0)

        self.recognitionRequest = nil
        self.recognitionTask = nil

        self.recordButton.isEnabled = true
        self.recordButton.setTitle("Start
Recording", for: [])
    }
}
```

The availability of speech recognition services should be constantly checked upon. For some languages, speech recognition runs on Apple servers, which requires a stable Internet connection. In case the Internet connection gets lost, your app should be ready to manage the disruption of service that may happen.

Any time speech recognition services become unavailable, the SFSpeechRecognizer object activates its delegate.

SpokenWord provides a delegate object and executes the speechRecognizer(_:availabilityDidChange:) method to respond to availability changes. When services become unavailable, the method disables the Start Recording button and updates its title. Once services become available, the method reenables the button and restores its original title:

```
public func speechRecognizer(_
speechRecognizer: SFSpeechRecognizer,
availabilityDidChange available: Bool) {
    if available {
        recordButton.isEnabled = true
        recordButton.setTitle("Start
Recording", for: [])
    } else {
        recordButton.isEnabled = false
        recordButton.setTitle("Recognition
Not Available", for: .disabled)
    }
}
```

Sound Analysis

Sound Analysis is a great feature that enables users to classify various sounds by examining audio files and streams.

You can spot and save various sounds in your app by creating an SNClassifySoundRequest to analyze an audio file or stream. A single sound request can identify over 300 sounds. Alternatively, you can identify a custom set of sounds by providing the sound request with a custom Core

ML model. You do that by creating an MLSoundClassifier with audio data in Create ML and including the following models:

- **Audio Analyzers:** Help to identify individual sounds in a file, such as a recording, with an audio file analyzer.

  - **class SNAudioFileAnalyzer:** An analyzer that runs sound classification requests on an audio file.

  - **class SNAudioStreamAnalyzer:** An object you create to analyze a stream of audio data and provide the results to your app.

- **Sound Classification Requests:** Applied to detect and identify hundreds of sounds by using a trained classifier.

  - **class SNClassifySoundRequest:** A request that classifies sound using a Core ML model.

  - **class SNClassificationResult:** A result that contains the highest-ranking classifications in a time range.

Classifying Sounds in an Audio File

By processing audio files with an SNAudioFileAnalyzer you can recognize different sounds as they occur in a recording. For instance, a sound recording app can activate an audio file analyzer to set searchable metadata tags to each sound sample in its library. The same app could also utilize the analyzer to attach timestamps to each recording so that the user can scroll to a moment with a necessary sound.

You forward a primary Sound Classification Request by passing a version identifier to the init(classifierIdentifier:) initializer:[6]

```
let version1 = SNClassifierIdentifier.
version1
let request = try
SNClassifySoundRequest(classifierIdentifier:
version1)
```

It is then required of you to create an instance of the model's wrapper class. Xcode automatically produces a class with the same name (minus the mlmodel extension) and passes the instance's model property to the init(mlModel:) initializer:

```
// Use a default model configuration.
let defaultConfig = MLModelConfiguration()

// Create an instance of the sound
classifier's wrapper class.
let soundClassifier = try
SoundClassifier(configuration:
defaultConfig)

// Create a classify sound request that
uses the custom sound classifier.
let request = try
SNClassifySoundRequest(mlModel:
soundClassifier.model)
```

---

[6] https://developer.apple.com/documentation/soundanalysis/classifying_sounds_in_an_audio_file, Apple

You can then implement a type that receives results from an audio analyzer by following the SNResultsObserving protocol. The protocol determines the methods an analyzer calls as it processes results or errors, or when it finishes a task:

```
let resultsObserver = ResultsObserver()
/// An observer that receives results from
a classify sound request.
class ResultsObserver: NSObject,
SNResultsObserving {
    /// Notifies the observer when a
request generates a prediction.
    func request(_ request: SNRequest,
didProduce result: SNResult) {

        // Downcast the result to a
classification result.
        guard let result = result as?
SNClassificationResult else  { return }

        // Get the prediction with the
highest confidence.
        guard let classification = result.
classifications.first else { return }

        // Get the starting time.
        let timeInSeconds = result.
timeRange.start.seconds

        // Convert the time to a human-
readable string.
        let formattedTime = String(format:
"%.2f", timeInSeconds)
        print("Analysis result for audio
at time: \(formattedTime)"
```

```
        // Convert the confidence to a
percentage string.
        let percent = classification.
confidence * 100.0
        let percentString = String(format:
"%.2f%%", percent)

        // Print the classification's name
(label) with its confidence.
        print("\(classification.
identifier): \(percentString)
confidence.\n")
    }
    /// Notifies the observer when a
request generates an error.
    func request(_ request: SNRequest,
didFailWithError error: Error) {
        print("The the analysis failed: \
(error.localizedDescription)")
    }
    /// Notifies the observer when a
request is complete.
    func requestDidComplete(_ request:
SNRequest) {
        print("The request completed
successfully!")
    }
}
```

The observer in this example displays the prediction's outcome may it be a timestamp, a classification name, to the console. You may then set your observer to take action that is suitable for your app according to that result. At the same time, it is important that you remember to maintain a strong reference to your observer since sound analyzers do not keep strong references to your observer by default.

When it comes to creating an Audio File Analyzer you do that by introducing the SNAudioFileAnalyzer and passing a URL to an audio file to the init(url:) initializer:

```
/// Creates an analyzer for an audio file.
/// - Parameter audioFileURL: The URL to
an audio file.
func createAnalyzer(audioFileURL: URL) ->
SNAudioFileAnalyzer? {
    return try? SNAudioFileAnalyzer(url:
audioFileURL)
}
```

It is also worth mentioning that Audio file analyzers operate with any compressed or uncompressed audio file format that Core Audio supports. You should add your sound classification request and results in observer to the analyzer by calling the add(_:withObserver:) method:[7]

```
// Create a new observer to receive
notifications for analysis results.
resultsObserver = ResultsObserver()

// Prepare a new request for the trained
model.
let request = try
SNClassifySoundRequest(mlModel: model)
try audioFileAnalyzer.add(request,
withObserver: resultsObserver)
```

---

[7] https://developer.apple.com/documentation/soundanalysis/classifying_sounds_in_an_audio_file, Apple

```
Start analyzing the audio file by calling
the analyze() or
analyze(completionHandler:) methods.
```

```
// Analyze the audio data.
audioFileAnalyzer.analyze()
```

Once processed, audio analyzer sends each result to your SNResultsObserving instance in the following format:

Analysis result for audio at time: 1.45

Acoustic Guitar: 90.39% confidence.

…

Analysis result for audio at time: 8.74

Acoustic Guitar: 50.45% confidence.

…

Analysis result for audio at time: 14.15

Tambourine: 77.39% confidence.

…

Analysis result for audio at time: 20.92

Snare Drum: 50.87% confidence.

VISION

The Vision framework is applied to complete face and face landmark detection, text detection, barcode recognition, image registration, and general feature searching. Vision also permits the use of custom Core ML models for tasks like classification or object detection. It includes to following key models in its algorithms set:[8]

- **Essentials:** Used to generate a feature print to figure the distance between images:

  - **class VNRequest:** The abstract superclass for analysis requests.

  - **class VNImageBasedRequest:** The abstract superclass for image analysis requests that focus on a specific part of an image.

  - **class VNClassifyImageRequest:** A request to classify an image.

  - **class VNGenerateImageFeaturePrintRequest:** An image-based request to generate feature prints from an image.

  - **class VNImageRequestHandler:** An object that processes one or more image analysis requests pertaining to a single image.

  - **class VNObservation:** The abstract superclass for analysis results.

- **Image Sequence Analysis:** Applied to create image masks for people automatically by using semantic person-segmentation:

  - **class VNStatefulRequest:** An abstract request type that builds evidence of a condition over time.

---

[8] https://developer.apple.com/documentation/vision, Apple

- **class VNGeneratePersonSegmentationRequest:**
  An object that produces a matte image for a person that it finds in the input image.

- **class VNDetectDocumentSegmentationRequest:**
  An object that detects rectangular regions that contain text in the input image.

- **class VNSequenceRequestHandler:** An object that processes image analysis requests for each frame in a sequence.

- **Saliency Analysis**

  - **class VNGenerateAttentionBasedSaliencyImageRequest:** An object that produces a heat map that identifies the parts of an image most likely to draw attention.

  - **class VNGenerateObjectnessBasedSaliencyImageRequest:** A request that generates a heat map that identifies the parts of an image most likely to represent objects.

  - **class VNSaliencyImageObservation:** An observation that contains a grayscale heat map of important areas across an image.

- **Object Tracking**

  - **class VNTrackingRequest:** The abstract superclass for image analysis requests that track unique features across multiple images or video frames.

- **class VNTrackRectangleRequest:** An image analysis request that tracks the movement of a previously identified rectangular object across multiple images or video frames.

- **class VNTrackObjectRequest:** An image analysis request that tracks the movement of a previously identified object across multiple images or video frames.

- **class VNDetectedObjectObservation:** An observation that provides the position and extent of an image feature that an image analysis request detects.

- **Face and Body Detection**

  - **class VNDetectFaceCaptureQualityRequest:** A request that produces a floating-point number that represents the capture quality of a face in a photo.

  - **class VNDetectFaceLandmarksRequest:** An image analysis request that finds facial features like eyes and mouth in an image.

  - **class VNDetectFaceRectanglesRequest:** A request that finds faces within an image.

  - **class VNDetectHumanRectanglesRequest:** A request that finds rectangular regions that contain people in an image.

  - **class VNHumanObservation:** An object that represents a person that the request detects.

- **Body and Hand Pose Detection**

  - **class VNDetectHumanBodyPoseRequest:** A request that detects a human body pose.

  - **class VNDetectHumanHandPoseRequest:** A request that detects a human hand pose.

  - **class VNRecognizedPointsObservation:** An observation that provides the points the analysis recognized.

  - **class VNHumanBodyPoseObservation:** An observation that provides the body points the analysis recognized.

  - **class VNHumanHandPoseObservation:** An observation that provides the hand points the analysis recognized.

  - **class VNPoint:** An immutable object that represents a single, two-dimensional point in an image.

  - **class VNDetectedPoint:** An object that represents a normalized point in an image, along with a confidence value.

  - **class VNRecognizedPoint:** An object that represents a normalized point in an image, along with an identifier label and a confidence value.

  - **struct VNRecognizedPointKey:** The data type for all recognized point keys.

  - **struct VNRecognizedPointGroupKey:** The data type for all recognized point group keys.

- **Animal Detection**

  - **class VNRecognizeAnimalsRequest:** A request that recognizes animals in an image.

- **Trajectory Detection**

  - **class VNDetectTrajectoriesRequest:** A request that detects the trajectories of shapes moving along a parabolic path.

  - **class VNDetectContoursRequest:** A request that detects the contours of the edges of an image.

- **Text Detection**

  - **class VNDetectTextRectanglesRequest:** An image analysis request that finds regions of visible text in an image.

  - **class VNTextObservation:** Information about regions of text that an image analysis request detects.

  - **class VNRecognizeTextRequest:** An image analysis request that finds and recognizes text in an image.

  - **class VNRecognizedTextObservation:** A request that detects and recognizes regions of text in an image.

- **Image Alignment**

  - **class VNTargetedImageRequest:** The abstract superclass for image analysis requests that operate on both the processed image and a secondary image.

- **class VNImageRegistrationRequest:** The abstract superclass for image analysis requests that align images according to their content.

- **class VNTranslationalImageRegistrationRequest:** An image analysis request that determines the affine transform necessary to align the content of two images.

- **class VNHomographicImageRegistrationRequest:** An image analysis request that determines the perspective warp matrix necessary to align the content of two images.

- **class VNImageAlignmentObservation:** The abstract superclass for image analysis results that describe the relative alignment of two images.

- **class VNImageTranslationAlignmentObservation:** Affine transform information that an image alignment request produces.

- **class VNImageHomographicAlignment Observation:** An object that represents a perspective warp transformation.

Tracking the User's Face in Real-Time

Now let us see how you can actually detect and track faces from the selfie feed in real-time. This section will show how to create requests to track human faces and review the results of those requests. In order to analyze the geometry of searched facial features, the code draws paths around the primary detected face and its most notable features. The sample app provides a few key computer vision algorithms to find a face in the image. Once it finds a face, it tries to track that face across every other frame. Finally, using Core Animation layers, it places a green box around the observed face, as well as yellow paths where facial features are located.

First things first, you need to set up a camera capture session using delegates to prepare images for Vision. Configuring the camera involves the following steps. First, you should create a new AVCaptureSession to represent video capture. Then channel its output through AVCaptureSession and set the user's input device by specifying its resolution and camera type.

Next, you might want to create a serial dispatch queue that would ensure that video frames, received asynchronously through delegate callback methods, are delivered in order. You can then establish a capture session with AVMediaType video to be able to set its device and resolution. Finally, it is necessary to designate the video's preview layer and add it to your view hierarchy, so the camera knows where to display video frames as they are captured.

It is also possible to place a completion handler for a Vision request handler to activate when it finishes. The completion handler suggests whether the request succeeded or failed. If the request succeeded, its results property would hold data specific to the type of request that you can apply to identify the object's current location.

In case you are dealing with face rectangle requests, the VNFaceObservation provided via callback has a bounding box for each detected face. The sample utilizes this bounding box to draw lines around each of the detected face platforms on top of the preview image:[9]

[9] https://developer.apple.com/documentation/vision/tracking_the_user_s_face_in_real_time, Apple

```swift
let faceDetectionRequest = VNDetectFaceRec
tanglesRequest(completionHandler: {
(request, error) in
    if error != nil {
        print("FaceDetection error: \
(String(describing: error)).")
    }
    guard let faceDetectionRequest =
request as? VNDetectFaceRectanglesRequest,
        let results = faceDetectionRequest.
results as? [VNFaceObservation] else {
            return
    }
    DispatchQueue.main.async {
        // Add the observations to the
tracking list
        for observation in results {
            let faceTrackingRequest = VNTr
ackObjectRequest(detectedObjectObservat
ion: observation)
            requests.
append(faceTrackingRequest)
        }
        self.trackingRequests = requests
    }
})
```

In addition to drawing paths, you can access specific facial-feature data such as eye, pupil, nose, and lip parameters in the face observation's items list. Your app can process this information to track the user's face and apply various custom effects.

Moreover, you can complete any image preprocessing in the delegate method fileOutput(_:didOutputSampleBuffer:from:). In this delegate method, establish a pixel buffer to hold image contents, set the device's orientation, and check whether you have a face to track. But before the Vision framework can track an object, it should first know which object to track. You can decide which face to track first by creating a VNImageRequestHandler and passing it a still image frame. In the case of video, forward individual frames to the request handler as they arrive in the delegate method fileOutput(_:didOutputSampleBuffer:from:):

```
let imageRequestHandler = VNImageRequestHa
ndler(cvPixelBuffer: pixelBuffer,
           orientation: exifOrientation,
           options: requestHandlerOptions)
do {
    guard let detectRequests = self
.detectionRequests else {
        return
    }
    try imageRequestHandler.
perform(detectRequests)
} catch let error as NSError {
    NSLog("Failed to perform
FaceRectangleRequest: %@", error)
}
```

In this example, the VNImageRequestHandler is great for managing the detection of faces and objects in still images, but it cannot carry information from one frame to the next.

Once you get an observation from the image request handler's face detection, you should input it to the sequence request handler:

```
try self.sequenceRequestHandler.
perform(requests,
            on: pixelBuffer,
            orientation: exifOrientation)
```

If the detector has not found a face, create another image request handler to detect a face. When that detection succeeds, and you have a face observation, track it by creating the following VNTrackObjectRequest:

```
// Setup the next round of tracking.
var newTrackingRequests =
[VNTrackObjectRequest]()
for trackingRequest in requests {
    guard let results = trackingRequest.
results else {
        return
    }
    guard let observation = results[0]
as? VNDetectedObjectObservation else {
        return
    }
        if !trackingRequest.isLastFrame {
        if observation.confidence > 0.3 {
            trackingRequest
.inputObservation = observation
        } else {
```

```
            trackingRequest.isLastFrame =
true
        }
        newTrackingRequests
.append(trackingRequest)
    }
}
```

When you are done with this final part, you need to call the sequence handler's perform(_:) function. Since this method runs synchronously, you should use a background queue to avoid blocking the main queue as it implements, and call back to the main queue only if you need to perform critical user interface (UI) updates.

DETECTING OBJECTS BY CORE ML AND VISION

Detecting objects by Core ML is done with models that are integrated into Xcode projects. You can select different versions of models to optimize for sizes and architectures:

- **FCRN-DepthPrediction:** Used to predict the depth of a single image.

- **MOST:** Applies to classify a single handwritten digit (supports digits 0–9).

- **UpdatableDrawingClassifier:** Standard drawing classifier that learns to recognize new drawings based on a K-Nearest Neighbors model (KNN).

- **MobileNetV2:** The MobileNetv2 architecture set to classify the dominant object in a camera frame or image.

- **Resnet50:** A Residual Neural Network is used to identify the dominant object in a camera frame or image.

- **SqueezeNet:** A small Deep Neural Network architecture that classifies the dominant object in a camera frame or image.

- **DeeplabV3:** Used to split the pixels of a camera frame or image into a predefined set of classes.

- **YOLOv3:** Great model to locate and classify around 80 different types of objects present in a camera frame or image.

- **PostNet:** Can estimates up to 17 joint positions for each person in an image.

- **BERT-SQuAD:** Used to review text and find answers to questions about it.

When it comes to the Vision framework detecting objects in still images, you can rely on it to process rectangles, faces, text, and barcodes at any orientation. In this section, we shall see how to create requests to detect these types of objects and interpret the results of those requests. In order to help you visualize where an observation occurs, and how it looks, the sample code we present will use Core Animation layers to draw paths around detected features in images.

In order to see the following sample in action, you need to first build and run the project, then use the toggle switches to select which kinds of objects (any combination of rectangles, faces, barcodes, and text) to detect.

The sample then uses computer vision algorithms to look for the desired features in the provided image. Finally, the sample draws colored paths around observed features on Core Animation layers.

Vision processes still image-based requests using a VNImageRequestHandler and assumes that images are oriented upright, so you should forward your image with that orientation in mind. As a rule, you can initialize a VNImageRequestHandler from image data in the following formats:[10]

- **CGImage:** The Core Graphics image format, retrievable from any UIImage through its helper method cgImage. You can specify orientation through the initializer using CGImagePropertyOrientation.

- **CIImage:** The Core Image format, best used if you already have Core Image in your image processing pipeline. CIImage objects do not hold orientation, so you have to supply it in the initializer init(ciImage:or ientation:options:).

- **CVPixelBuffer:** The Core Video image format for data from a live feed and movies. CVPixelBuffer objects do not have a certain orientation, so supply it in the initializer init(cvPixelBuffer:orientation:options:).

- **NSData:** Image data compressed or placed in memory, as you might receive over a network connection.

---

[10] https://developer.apple.com/documentation/vision/detecting_objects_in_still_images, Apple

For instance, photos downloaded from a website or the cloud fall into this category. You need to make sure that all the images downloaded from the web have upright orientation; if they do not, inform Vision about the orientation through the initializer init(data:orientation:options:).

- **NSURL:** A URL path to the image on disk.

Vision may not process sideways or upside-down features properly if it sees the wrong orientation. Photos selected in the sample's image picker typically hold orientation information and you can access this data through the UIImage property imageOrientation. In case you acquire your photos through other means, such as the web or other apps, you need to make sure to check for orientation and provide it separately if it does not come combined with the image.

You should start detecting objects with the proper vision request using VNImageRequestHandler in the following manner:

```
// Create a request handler.
let imageRequestHandler =
VNImageRequestHandler(cgImage: image,
                orientation: orientation,
                options: [:])
```

If you are required to make multiple requests from the same image (like detecting facial features as well as faces), create and combine all requests to pass into the image request handler. Vision will run each request and process its completion handler on its own thread.

Alternatively, you can pair each request with a completion handler to operate request-specific code after Vision is done with all requests. The following sample draws boxes differently based on the type of request, so this code differs from request to request:[11]

```
lazy var rectangleDetectionRequest:
VNDetectRectanglesRequest = {
    let rectDetectRequest = VNDetectRectan
glesRequest(completionHandler: self.
handleDetectedRectangles)
    // Customize & configure the request
to detect only certain rectangles.
    rectDetectRequest.maximumObservations =
8 // Vision currently supports up to 16.
    rectDetectRequest.minimumConfidence =
0.6 // Be confident.
    rectDetectRequest.minimumAspectRatio =
0.3 // height / width
    return rectDetectRequest
}()
```

When you are have created all your requests, you can pass them as an array to the request handler's synchronous perform(_:). Vision computations typically take some time, so make sure to use a background queue to avoid blocking the main queue as it operates:

---

[11] https://developer.apple.com/documentation/vision/detecting_objects_in_ still_images, Apple

```
// Send the requests to the request
handler.
DispatchQueue.global(qos: .userInitiated).
async {
    do {
        try imageRequestHandler.
perform(requests)
    } catch let error as NSError {
        print("Failed to perform image
request: \(error)")
        self.presentAlert("Image Request
Failed", error: error)
        return
    }
}
```

As a result, the method perform(_:) is expected to return a Boolean representing whether the requests succeeded or resulted in an error. If it succeeded, its results property holds observation or tracking information, such as a detected object's location and bounding box. You can access results in two ways:

- By checking the results property after calling perform(_:).

- In the VNImageBasedRequest object's completion handler, using the callback's observation parameter to access detection information. The callback results may hold multiple observations, so examine each observation array carefully.

To illustrate, the following sample draws facial observations and their landmarks' bounding boxes to locate the features and draw a rectangle around them:[12]

```
// Perform drawing on the main thread.
DispatchQueue.main.async {
    guard let drawLayer = self.pathLayer,
        let results = request?.results as?
[VNFaceObservation] else {
            return
    }
    self.draw(faces: results,
onImageWithBounds: drawLayer.bounds)
    drawLayer.setNeedsDisplay()
}
```

Even if Vision calls its completion handlers on a background thread, it is advised to dispatch UI calls like the path-drawing code to the main thread. Normally, access to UIKit, AppKit, and resources should be serialized, so changes that affect the app's immediate interface belong on the main thread:

```
transaction.begin()
for observation in faces {
    let faceBox = boundingBox(forRegionOfI
nterest: observation.boundingBox,
withinImageBounds: bounds)
```

---

[12] https://developer.apple.com/documentation/vision/detecting_objects_in_still_images, Apple

```
    let faceLayer = shapeLayer(color:
.yellow, frame: faceBox)

    // Add to pathLayer on top of image.
    pathLayer?.addSublayer(faceLayer)
}
CATransaction.commit()
```

In order to process face landmark requests, the detector provides VNFaceObservation results with greater detail, such as VNFaceLandmarkRegion2D. For explicit text observations, you can locate individual characters by examining the characterBoxes property. And if you are dealing with barcode observations, some supported symbologies have payload information in the payloadStringValue property, letting you parse the components of detected barcodes. Similar to a supermarket scanner, barcode detection is optimized for reading one barcode per image.

It is usually up to your assignment requirements to see if you need to use or store data from the observations before exiting the completion handler. Instead of drawing paths like in the above-mentioned code sample, you can write your own custom code to extract what your app needs from each observation.

In order to avoid unnecessary computation, it is recommended to create all your requests before querying Vision, collect them in a requests array, and submit that array in a single step. And if you need to perform detection across multiple, random images, you may create a separate image handler for each image and make requests to each handler on separate threads, so they operate in parallel. Each image request handler takes additional processing time and memory, so it is best to keep them away from the main thread. Instead, dispatch these handlers on additional background threads, calling back to the main thread only for crucial UI updates such as displaying images.

That brings us to the end of this chapter, wherein we have covered at length topics such as ML with Swift.

Appraisal

In 2010, a small team at Google started working on making Swift the first mainstream language with first-class language-integrated programming capacities. The reach and initial results of the project have been rather outstanding, and general public usability has only proved that. Since then, the Swift programming language has caused colossal waves of change in iOS app development. Swift was officially announced by Tim Cook, CEO of Apple in 2014. Back then, Tim Cook described Swift as "the next big programming language" and predicted that iOS developers worldwide would rely on it for the next 20 years. Today, Swift programming language is not only a happy-end story that Tim said it would be, but it also aims to become the future for iOS app developers. In fact, Swift has already seized the majority of the market since its arrival. But, if you are an iOS app developer who still thinks otherwise, this book will hopefully help change your mind.

Learning to program is a fascinating, interactive process between your program and you. Just like learning to play any musical instrument, you need to practice. You are expected to work through the examples and exercises in this book. Reading about a concept does not necessarily mean

DOI: 10.1201/9781003254089-8

you know how to apply it and use it. You will learn a lot from working through the exercises in this book. However, you can really master a language only when you debug your programs. Spending time walking through your code and finding out why it is not operating the way you want is an exceptional learning process. As a new developer, at times, you might find it frustrating, you could end up questioning why you are doing this, and whether you are good enough to solve the problem. Programming could be humbling, even for the most experienced developer. Yet like with most things in life, the more you practice, the better you get. And by practicing, we mean programming. You can achieve great things as a programmer. Seeing your app in the App Store is surely one of the most fulfilling accomplishments. However, there is a price to pay for that, and that is all the time you have to put in learning and coding.

This book starts with introducing the main logic concepts in Swift Playgrounds and then examines those concepts to Xcode. Typically, most students are visual or prefer to learn by doing. Both techniques are used here. We shall walk you through topics and concepts with visual examples and then take you through step-by-step examples reviewing the concepts. The same topics are often repeated in different chapters to lock what you have learned and apply these skills in new formats. This is a proven method to enable new programmers to reapply development skills and experience a sense of accomplishment as they grow.

We shall walk you through the process of comprehending the development process for your iOS apps and show what technologies you need. These are the key iOS development technologies you will have to learn in order to build a successful app and get it on the App Store: iOS Software Development Kit, Object-Oriented Programming, Xcode Integrated Development Environment (IDE), Debugging, Performance Tuning, as well as Apple Developer web site and App Analytics.

A whole chapter would be dedicated to Xcode as it has all of the tools needed to create an app within one software package: a text editor, a compiler, and a build system. With Xcode, you can script, compile, and debug your app, and once you are finished, you can forward it to the Apple app store. Xcode holds a number of tools to help the development process move smoothly so that developers can create apps lightning faster, and beginners could avoid uncertainty and barriers to start their application.

Basically, this tool is designed to give you one window in which to operate as a developer. It has a source code checker and autocomplete features that will make writing source code much easier. Once you are ready for a new project, you can select from the available templates and stored snippets of code to acquire a basic foundation on which to build. Alternatively, you can even create your templates if you find you are frequently retyping commonly-applied code. These great features let beginners use these templates to work on their app even if they have little knowledge of application development. At the same time, advanced developers will also find these features helpful to streamline their assignment and make the application development process much trouble-free.

The Apple guides encourage you to investigate the technologies in the Cocoa Touch layer to see whether they meet your needs before looking at other tools. The Cocoa Touch layer holds most of the object-oriented developer-facing frameworks for building iOS applications. In other words, Apple desires for Cocoa Touch to be your single point of entry into iOS app development. Both the Cocoa Touch framework and the Foundation framework described in this book make up the two critical iOS development components used by developers.

To put it simply, Cocoa Touch is where you are going to build your app's user interface, manage touch-based and gesture-based interactions, link the user interface to the app's data, regulate the general multitasking, and integrate everything from state preservation to push notification to printing. Moreover, Cocoa Touch offers object-oriented access for managing your address book and events, building games, and dealing with ads, maps, messages, and social media. Most of the time, you will work through Cocoa Touch because it provides almost instant access to the other layers of the technology. In particular, you will manipulate with the UIKit framework, which packages most of the operability just mentioned.

One of the most extraordinary things about developing iOS apps is that almost everything is free to start creating your app. Core ML framework is exactly one of those things. It delivers high-speed performance with simple integration of machine learning models, letting you build apps with sophisticated new features using just a few lines of code. Once you master Core ML, you can easily add pre-built machine learning features into your apps using Application Programming Interface (APIs) or use Create ML for more transparency and train custom Core ML models right on your Mac. It is also possible to convert models from other training libraries using Core ML Converters or download ready-to-use Core ML models.

This book also includes chapters covering user interface handling, view transitions, and features tracking. Chapters are also provided explaining how to combine SwiftUI views with existing UIKit-based projects and describes the integration process of UIKit code into SwiftUI. The Swift standard library could also be perceived as the framework that consists of the core components, tools, and types to help build your Swift apps. And before you start building your own custom data structures, it is essential to understand the primary data structures that the Swift standard library holds. We shall primarily focus on Strings, Ints, Floats, Bools, Array, Dictionary, and Set.

Along the way, the topics covered in this book are put into practice through detailed code samples and source codes. User interface design mostly involves gathering together various items and laying them out on the screen in a way that provides a smooth and intuitive user experience. It is important to remember that user interface layouts should also be responsive so that they appear correctly on any device regardless of screen size and device orientation. To facilitate user interface layout design, SwiftUI offers several layout views and components to choose from. In this book, we have looked at some standard layout stack views and suitable frames. By default, a view has to be sized regarding its content and the restrictions imposed on it by any view in which it may be contained. When there isn't enough space is available, a view could be restricted in size resulting in abbreviated content. For greater control of the space allocated to a view, a flexible frame could be the best suit to apply to the view.

Having provided these disclaimers, one might conclude that Swift is a great language, and the new additions are so original that it will undoubtedly find its place in the developers and machine learning communities. Therefore, if you want to contribute to such movements with enormous growth potential, now is a great time to start. Things are not yet fully established. Many services still need producing, and a small personal project now could become a considerable community force in the future as the Swift ecosystem continues to evolve and advance.

Index

Printed in the United States
by Baker & Taylor Publisher Services